Bob Cooper was born and educated in Western Australia; he has delivered his Outback Safety and Wilderness Survival courses for thirty years and is considered a leading survival instructor in Australia. He has honed his survival skills by learning from traditional cultures in Australia, Africa, North America and Malaysia.

Bob conducts survival courses for government agencies, private companies and the general public throughout Australia and is supported by an experienced team of instructors.

Bob Cooper Outback Survival offers survival merchandise and courses in the following subjects:

- Wilderness Survival
- Snake Handling
- SAR Tracking
- Team Building
- Survival Tool Making
- Personal Development
- Advanced Outback Survival

GW00808310

Information from www.bobcoopersurvival.com
Contact Bob at info@bobcoopersurvival.com

# OUTBACK SURVIVAL

- Survival kits
- Finding water and shelter
- Bush tucker
- Snakes and spiders
- Dealing with fear

# BOB COOPER
## AUSTRALIA'S LEADING SURVIVAL EXPERT

hachette AUSTRALIA

## Disclaimer

Information and advice in this book is of a general nature, and you should always seek specific advice for your own particular situation.

## ⌐ᴴ hachette
AUSTRALIA

Published in Australia and New Zealand in 2012
by Hachette Australia
(an imprint of Hachette Australia Pty Limited)
Level 17, 207 Kent Street, Sydney NSW 2000
www.hachette.com.au

10 9 8 7 6 5 4 3 2 1

National Library of Australia
Cataloguing-in-Publication data

Cooper, Bob.
   Outback survival / Bob Cooper.
   9780733628313 (pbk.)
   Wilderness survival – Australia. Outdoor life – Australia.
   Survivial – Australia.
613.690994

Cover concept by Xou Creative
Cover by Seymour Designs
Text design by Seymour Designs
Drawings by Lazar Radanovich

Typeset in ITC Officiana Serif by Kirby Jones
Printed in Australia by Griffin Press, Adelaide, an Accredited ISO AS/
NZS 4001:2004 Environmental Management Systems printer

# CONTENTS

# FOREWORD

Survival and bushcraft have always been part of the Australian culture and psyche. Early pioneers, explorers and stockmen were dependent on their ability to read and adapt to nature. Their survival, success and wellbeing hinged on their ability to observe and change. People who were able to survive and learn from nature stayed alive and were successful. If not they suffered, went broke or perished. Their stories form part of the mythology of Australia, immortalised in the stories and poetry of Paterson, Lawson and others. Before them, the many Aboriginal Nations of Australia were grand masters of survival and bushcraft, creating the longest enduring civilisation and culture on earth, using only what they could from nature.

In more recent times we have become increasingly removed from the daily need for bushcraft and survival skills, and yet it still holds a fascination for us. 'Reality' TV shows have sensationalised and packaged survival for entertainment and mass-market appeal. The result is designed to entertain rather than inform and the survival advice in such shows is questionable.

Bob Cooper established his business in the mid-1980s. Since then he has been providing high quality educational experiences for an international audience. His survival courses are recognised as among the best in the world, and have regularly been the subject of local and international documentaries. In *Outback Survival*, Bob candidly tells his story about how he came to be one of the world's leading survival specialists and then goes on to outline his philosophy and strategies of survival.

I have had the pleasure of instructing with Bob since 1995 and I have learnt a vast amount from him. I have walked in excess of 1000 kilometres in the Pilbara region of Australia as both a participant and instructor on Bob's courses, and on each trip I learn more from him. I am humbled and awed by the extent of his knowledge. His masterful approach to teaching allows Bob to scan the environment, the group he is with and his extensive knowledge, bringing it all together in a way that makes the most of every learning opportunity. He is himself a perpetual student, constantly learning from the environment, his students and other masters of his craft.

Bob studies the tragedies of the outback – deaths resulting from a lack of skill or knowledge – seeking to understand what led the person to make the decisions they made, and what knowledge would have helped them. The story of Oyers Panders recounted in this book shows the level of respect and care Bob shows for these victims of tragedy, and the lengths he will take to understand and pass on the lessons to be learnt.

He is also an avid experimenter, constantly seeking new and different ways to do things. On one of our recent courses, Bob was experimenting with boiling water in a plastic bottle over an open fire. He had read this was possible and tried it once before, and wanted to refine his technique, all the while teaching his instructors and students. The resulting lesson was fascinating, entertaining and intensely practical. That knowledge and skill are outlined in this book.

That is the nature of the man. Bob is not content to read or hear about something and assume it will work. His extensive know-how has been hard-won by trialling and refining in actual survival situations as well as created scenarios. He will not teach something until he understands it and can duplicate the results over and over again – one day someone's life may depend on it, and Bob takes that responsibility very seriously.

As a result, *Outback Survival* is a remarkable accomplishment. You can be assured that the techniques and skills in this book have been tried and tested in many situations and environments by Bob personally, his instructors and his students. Not only that, but they have been found to be consistently effective and potentially lifesaving. The knowledge and information in this book represents Bob's lifetime of learning and refining his own skills and equipment along with over two decades of teaching those skills to others. You would do well to take a leaf out of Bob's book – study what he has to say, and then play, experiment and practise. While many of Bob's strategies are simple, they are not easy to learn in a real-life survival situation. Time spent on practice will always be time well spent, significantly increasing your chances of survival if you ever need to apply your skills for real.

Even if you never use the ideas in this book in a genuine survival situation, you will find much of the wisdom applies broadly to all areas of life. I have personally found benefits in my personal and business relationships, planning events for recreation, holidays here and abroad, and personal confidence and satisfaction from what I have learnt from Bob.

My wish for you the reader is that you are inspired to explore the outback and to back yourself with the skills to plan well and deal with any mishaps. I hope that your survival experience is limited to practice rather than actual events. And with any luck I'll meet you out on the track or on one of Bob's excellent courses.

Enjoy *Outback Survival*.

Mike House
Survival Instructor

# INTRODUCTION

Over the years I have witnessed and felt the fear of death during potentially fatal land, sea and air mishaps. Survival skills can replace fear with respect for, and trust in, nature. Such knowledge enables people to walk freely and be nurtured by the 'soul food' provided by the natural environment.

Many irrational fears cloud people's engagement with our outback – and even in the bushlands of suburbia. The fears of snakes, spiders, being lost or alone are all acquired fears. Knowledge is the key to dispelling them and replacing that emotion with respect. As a society we need to recapture the survival skills and empathy with nature our ancestors instinctively knew. True appreciation and understanding of our natural environment may be the only factor that saves it and, on occasion, us.

This book is my contribution to this necessary new awareness.

Bob Cooper

# PART 1
# MY STORY

# Chapter 1
# EARLY DAYS

At the time of writing I am 57 years old and have been instructing in bush survival for more than 30 years. Most of my early courses were conducted in one of the most remote and hottest parts of the world, the eastern Pilbara Region of Western Australia, also known as the Western Desert. It remains the most isolated place on earth.

When I am introduced to people as a survival instructor, I always get asked two questions: 'How did you get started in that?' and 'How do you become a survival instructor?'

The answers follow.

I was 17 when I put myself on my first survival challenge – although I didn't know it at the time. My idea was to walk along the coastline to Yanchep, then a tiny coastal town about 65 kilometres north of Perth, and explore the national park during the summer school holidays. My map was the front page from a 1970 street directory with no roads marked beyond my starting point until Yanchep, and my provisions were 2 litres of water, lots of tinned food, a loaf of bread and a sleeping bag, all stuffed into a shoulder-strap navy kitbag. I was driven to the end of the coast road where the metropolitan area finished, hopped out and started walking along the beach leading north, unaware and unafraid of anything.

As the day grew hotter, however, things changed. By lunchtime it was 38°C, I had drunk all my water and my legs were sunburnt from wearing shorts. I was starting to feel unwell and I was very concerned about having no water left. The tinned food weighed me down, making walking on beach sand arduous, so by late afternoon I had buried 90 per cent of my tucker on top of a sand dune, marking the spot for future recovery (it's still all there). That night as I lay in the cool, soft sand dunes, my body dehydrated, legs and face burning and lips painfully blistered, I felt afraid and very alone. I knew there was no road to opt out on, and therefore no help. I had told my mother I'd hitchhike back to Perth from Yanchep in a week's time, so no one was coming to look for me for at least a week. The more I thought about that, the more I realised that I was in deep trouble, having no water and not knowing if there was any ahead of me. In my ignorance I waited until sunrise to move off, so missed a few hours of really cool walking time, which would have saved some sweat.

By 10 a.m. the hot easterly wind was in full force at 25 knots, blowing the bleached white sand so hard that it actually stung as it sandblasted my sunburnt legs. The effort to walk on the firm, wet sand was becoming harder and harder in my weakening, dehydrated condition. The sun was hot again and there was zero shade. It was at that point I realised that I could perish. At that exact dismal moment I don't know what made me look up to my right but I did – and thank all the gods, I spotted the roof of a shack. It was a squatter's fishing shack hidden behind the first line of sand dunes, with a rainwater tank on the side. What a lifesaver: water and shade! I drank so much water I felt sick.

I went inside the shack and made a cup of black coffee on the gas stove, which ran from cylinders outside, and then slept on one of the single-wire bunks until late afternoon. I robbed the rubbish bin of some old bottles, which I rinsed out, filled with water and departed a better and very grateful young man. That night I slept in the sand dunes, no longer as scared but still concerned, since I had absolutely no idea how far I had travelled. On day 3 I found several more shacks, topped up my water bottles and moved off again, arriving in Yanchep township around lunchtime.

In 1972 I passed out of fifth year high school with okay results and scored a job on a professional crayfish (lobster) boat as a 'deckie', living and working out of Lancelin with a German fisherman nicknamed Fritz. I changed boats three seasons later and experienced my first mayday on this boat, when the skipper crashed into a reef – missing the local Hole in the Wall channel by about 100 metres thanks to distraction.

The boat was on top of the reef and getting pounded by waves, but not breaking up; just wallowing like a stranded whale. The skipper sent a mayday over the radio, but a cray boat had spotted us and came to our aid. Our boat was rolling from side to side and on one of the down-rolls we jumped into waist-high water, then braced ourselves as the next wave hit the reef. It sent us washing across the reef into deep water, thankfully with only minor cuts, and then we were able to swim to the other boat.

I worked on several boats over a total of eight seasons, along the way obtaining my Master Class V and Master of Limited Trade Vessels skipper's tickets, and skippered a wet-line fishing boat, and a charter boat in the off-seasons. I've earned my fair share of stormy-sea stories and other disasters, one of the worst happening on the *Stacy Jay*, skippered by a terrific bloke, Les Cousins. Les's quick thinking and skills saved both our lives when we were hammered by a series of five big 'freak waves' while pulling pots in shallow waters.

The first wave hit us side-on with such force it catapulted eight 40-kilogram craypots off the deck and over the side of the boat. The next wave swamped us over the stern, flooding the deck and submerging me completely as I hung onto the tangled mess on the deck. But I still managed to cut loose the overboard pot ropes because the pots themselves were now acting as an anchor, making it impossible for the boat to manoeuvre. Our boat was sideways to the oncoming breakers, which is the most dangerous position of all, and wallowing with water. Les steered the boat by going with the surge and, when enough water had drained off, he turned it to face the next three 'green monsters'. They were sucking us forward and Les was idling the engine. Timing was the key: the boat needed just enough momentum to force its way up and over the wave, without crashing over the top. Not straight enough and we would roll the boat sideways; not enough speed and we would end-for-end it backwards.

I was on my feet to witness the battle: the last wave was the biggest. The roar of the surge was deafening and the sheer size was terrifying. As we climbed the face of a virtually sheer wall of water the wave's crest was feathering to begin its crashing blow. When we were nearly vertical, we started sliding backwards on our stern. At full speed the boat half-rose above the peak of the wave – then we fell like a stone into the vacuum behind it. I could hear the propeller scream as the stern shot up into the air and the front of the boat smashed into the trough. I lost my grip on the wheelhouse and was body-slammed into the deck, as was Les. Then he was back on his feet and we raced to safety out to sea, riding over the next looming swells. Out to sea meant out of danger – needless to say, we left the rest of the cray pots for another time. When we finally made it back to port later that morning, we drove straight to the local pub, still in our wet fishing clothes and beanies, and relived the story (several times).

# Chapter 2
# SPECIAL FORCES QUALIFIED

In 1978 I attended a YMCA bushcraft course and met instructors and other outdoor-education specialists. Then in 1979, with five of these like-minded men, I formed SABRE, the first survival and adventure-based company in Western Australia. One of those involved was Denis Reid, a Special Forces member. Thanks to Denis, in November 1981 I was accepted as a civilian to take part in a 26-day Special Air Service Regiment survival course. As a civvy, it was daunting to walk through the front gates of SASR HQ at Campbell Barracks on day 1 of four days of theory lectures. Senior instructor Warrant Officer Graham Brammer greeted us with: 'Welcome to the survival course, men. I designed this course and I am paid to be a bastard.' Something told me this was not going to be easy.

On day 2 I was taken to the Q Store and issued with two sets of greens to wear, a bush hat, and sleeping and cooking gear in a backpack. When the lectures finished our group of 21 participants (18 Aussie SASR men, two British

SF guys on exchange and one lone civvy – me) flew out of Pearse RAAF Base in a blacked-out Caribou cargo aircraft, landing several hours later somewhere in the outback: the practical phase had commenced. It certainly started with a shock: I didn't expect to be treated like a POW. We were threatened, ridiculed and made to strip naked and stand arms outstretched on a dirt track while a rubber-gloved medic performed a body search.

This treatment was designed to shake us into an uncomfortable emotional state and it worked for me. It was hot; I feared for my safety; I felt disorientated and intimidated. I got my boots and socks back but the next time I saw my clothes would be weeks later. We were each given two large, heavy jute sacks, one bag needle, a ball of string, a knife and 25 minutes to design an outfit to wear. It was a flat-out race to finish on time. I made a fetching 'Robin Hood' style hat with a matching dress made out of a single bag with a vee-cut front and a leg split on the right side. My ensemble included a carry-bag section on the back and a knife sheath on my hip. The next level up from uncomfortable would best describe my jute frock as it prickled its way into my skin with every movement and rasped on the more tender areas. We all had to perform a 'catwalk' parade in front of all the other participants and instructors – this was also a test of emotional control.

Then, as a well-dressed bunch of individuals, we were unceremoniously loaded into the back of a truck and driven to an unidentified location for the next phase, a solo navigation by the sun and stars. My watch was given back to me along with a hand-drawn 'mud map'. The objective was to find your way to checkpoints about

3 kilometres apart. At each checkpoint an instructor gave out the next bearing and distance, nothing else – and I mean *nothing* else. No words of encouragement or well wishes, just a stony-faced individual placing another X on my map – 'Go there'. Even after dark we continued, using the stars to find our 'cheerful' checkpoints.

At 19:30 hours, as I made my way along a track, I spotted a camp fire ahead at a T-junction: it had to be the checkpoint. Again, a lone instructor was there but this time I was told to sit and wait. One by one other hessian sacks arrived with varying degrees of cheerfulness. Some were totally silent.

'All right, you mob, get in,' we were told, as a truck pulled up next to us in a cloud of dust. In we filed like sheep and were transported to a set of old buildings. In the glare of lights powered by a nearby generator, I could see they were ruins. We lost our hessian clothes and watches and were each given a well-used shirt and long pants; no hat. We were loaded back onto the 'happy truck', driven somewhere and called out of the truck in groups of three. In the dark at the back of the truck we were given a medical kit and three knives, then instructed: 'Don't go more than 2 kilometres from this location – do you understand?' The instructor got back into the truck and drove off, its tail-lights fading in the powdery red dust.

'Piss off and don't come back!' one of the other guys yelled out. There was a long silence, then: 'Okay, I'm Mike.'

'I'm Bob.'

'And I'm Mal. Let's see what the bastards have left us.'

We could just make out that there was a variety of tablets and powders in small, sealed plastic bags but couldn't read the labels in the dark. In the silence we could hear a squeaking in the distance. We followed the sound to a windmill pumping fresh water into an old stone tank – that was a relief, as none of us had drunk since that morning. We drank directly out of the pipe that fed the tank, the least polluted option. We had no means of making a fire. No fire equals low morale, an increased sense of loneliness and little control over the 'now'.

We sat with our backs against one another to try to keep warm, but froze slowly until sunrise. One of the longest, coldest, darkest, most miserable nights I have ever spent in my entire life.

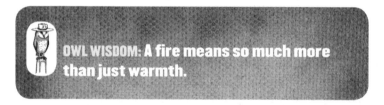

OWL WISDOM: A fire means so much more than just warmth.

Sunrise brought with it light and warmth. We walked back to the stone tank and discussed the value of our medical kit, and our immediate survival priorities.

To light a fire as soon as possible was top of the list. We knew we could light a fire by using the sugar coating off the antihistamine tablets mixed well with the antiseptic Condy's crystals then ground up – something that was taught in the theory phase. Mal's democratic idea was two long sticks and one short stick. I drew the short one – bugger. I only had one chance so I made sure that everything possible was done: found superfine dry tinder, scraped all the sugar coating off three tablets onto a flat tin windmill blade, added Condy's to a 50:50 composition and used a knife to grind the combination together. First a spark, then a flame, then – yahoo, guys, we have fire! We established a good base camp site on soft sand with a central fire, made a windbreak shelter out of old sheets of tin and branches, and slept close to the fire for warmth. We found a large rusty tin can in which to boil water and some old bottles for water storage. We purified the water with Condy's crystals.

For the next three days we survived on wattle seeds and a small snake.

Late afternoon on day 4, some goats arrived for a drink at the trough. We simply ran one down, a female with a kid. With my knife I dispatched the adult as humanely and respectfully as possible. Firstly we drank the milk, which we squeezed out of the mother's udder, before processing the carcass. We feasted on a mixed grill of organs and hindquarter. We hadn't eaten for more than four days, so you can imagine the morale boost of having a full stomach. The kid goat we kept alive and he adopted us, following us around like a puppy. We made him a collar and lead out of bootlaces and named him 'Son of Jerky', as we had sun-dried all the meat off the mother's carcass to preserve it. We did this by threading strips of meat onto fencing wire, which were hung on a stick tripod over a smoky fire. We ate it like that but also made a form of stew in our tins with wattle seeds and a side salad of native flax shoots.

On day 4 I made a chequers board out of an old piece of flat tin, colouring in the black squares using charcoal and using green wattle seeds and stones as pieces. The winner ate the seeds and the loser had to find more. I only played once with Mal, as he was feeling the mental pressure of being isolated and not knowing when this phase would end.

Mal's sadness turned into a real bad bout of depression on days 5 and 6. This dark period with Mal was very, very concerning. I had heartfelt sorrow for this bloke but neither Mike nor I had any idea of what to say or do; we just hoped he wouldn't suicide. On the seventh evening, around our humble camp fire, Mal shared his problems with us, telling us about his nightmares arising from two tours of Vietnam, his recent broken relationships and the agony of guilt that follows him. Mal slept well that night and awoke really cheerful and positive. All from just a few teary sentences told to people who listened and didn't judge. I realised that verbalising your concerns can help ease mental anguish.

About noon on day 8 the 'fun police' arrived to inspect what we had collectively and individually achieved. They took a photo of us and our adopted 'son' and that ended that phase. We didn't eat Son of Jerky. He was taken back to the homestead.

Once again we were politely transported away, picking up other groups en route and finally arriving at an old shearing shed with accommodation quarters. We had hot showers and didn't that warm water feel good. We dressed in our own clothes, then had a cooked meal of meat and vegies on a plate, using knives and forks – it felt almost lavish.

After our meal it was back to the serious stuff. We had a full Special Forces style briefing for the next three-day phase, which was a Combat Survival Patrol. Divided into two patrol groups, with every member carrying a weapon (one live round each), sleeping gear and three 24-hour ration packs, the objective was to reach an abandoned outstation 70 kilometres away within 72 hours. We were expected to forage en route to supplement the rations, through a mock war zone. W. O. Brammer selected a Captain as the patrol leader, with me as second in command (2IC) – I took on that role as an honour and an opportunity to test my leadership skills. With a fair bit of encouragement and lots of advice I believe I did a reasonable job, for a civvy.

Ten seconds after we headed out we were 'called' back by Brammer (he made two clicking sounds as there was no talking aloud in a 'war zone'). 'Nearly forgot, men,' he whispered. 'If any of you open your food ration packs you will all fail the entire course.' Yet another bastard of a psychological test, but I doubt it fazed any of us.

They walk fairly quickly, those SAS blokes, and we set up for the night at a predetermined spot 30 kilometres away. I had just gone to sleep in my sleeping bag when two of the fun police turned up and explained that some of the men hadn't successfully completed the navigation phase. So we all had to walk on a bearing of 22.5 degrees for 7.6 kilometres, using only the stars to find the target, a windmill marked on our map, and we had to do it now.

'What?!' As 2IC I had to make sure everyone was ready as soon as possible – which I did. As a group we shared the navigational task and arrived at the target some hours later. The instructors assessed us on arrival, then just walked off into the darkness. I suppose that meant we passed. So we re-established a camp and, for the second time that night, went to sleep. A pre-dawn start saw us reach our final destination, the old rundown outstation, by dark on day 2.

We had eaten only seeds and nuts en route, so the next morning we organised two hunting parties and by noon we were dining on emu meat barbecued on a corrugated-tin sheet hot plate. We slept very well that night.

At noon on the fourth day we were picked up and driven overnight to an isolated spot close to the coast. We were given natural visual boundaries to stay within, then, with limited gear, we started the most gruelling phase: to last more than three days without water – none was supplied and there was none in the vicinity. The best way to cope was to stay still in the shade and squeeze drops of water from the only available water source, a ground succulent called pigface. It tastes terrible but will save your life. We split into small groups and established our own resting areas. I teamed up with Terry, one of the Brits, and a PT instructor, another Bob. We walked a bit further than the rest of the group and found a limestone rock shelter, which meant we had 100 per cent shade. On day two, with my thirst only partially quenched by pigface juice, my tongue swelled, my kidneys hurt and none of us could speak properly. By day 3, just walking was a huge effort. But we managed to reach the prearranged RV point by 18.00 hours, as instructed. At 18.05 Graham informed us all that this 75th hour of the ordeal marked not only the end of this phase, but the course as well. We were jubilant, but you could hardly tell as we staggered over a small hill to a base camp and were given our kit and clobber back. We quenched our thirst on electrolytes in clean water, followed by bouts of vomiting from the first attempts to drink. Some men were worse than others. A few hours later we were all feeding on goat stew, feeling fine and glad to be alive. Then the course instructors, led by W. O. Brammer, delivered a thorough debrief and told us how we scored – I finished fifth out of the 21 men. I was later presented with an SAS Regiment certificate as a qualified Survival Instructor to military standards. As a civilian I accepted this proudly as an honour. Since then I have lectured on numerous SF survival courses and with visiting SF units from the UK, USA and Canada.

 **OWL WISDOM: Survival is a mind game. Never feel sorry for yourself in a predicament – and never get separated from your kit of essentials.**

# Chapter 3
# A REAL-LIFE SURVIVAL SITUATION

The next year, 1982, aged 28, I acted as a field assistant for anthropologists Kim Akerman and Peter Bindon who, with the help of the local Aboriginal community, were working in the Great Sandy Desert locating, classifying and recording the positions of significant Aboriginal sites for the Western Australian Museum. I was offered the position because Peter knew of my enthusiasm for bushcraft and survival.

Using hired 4WD vehicles we picked up elders from the Christmas Creek (Kurungal) and Balgo Mission (Wirrimanu) communities on the edge of the Western Desert region. With these 11 traditional elders we spent seven weeks venturing into areas of the desert, often where no white person had been before. The sheer beauty and magnificence of the desert in winter has to be seen to be believed – and we saw plenty.

Kim Akerman had been initiated into an Aboriginal tribe years before and he was an elder in Aboriginal eyes. Kim is well respected by the Aboriginal community and is entrusted with many of their rituals. This is sacred knowledge and I know of no other white person in such a privileged position. Two weeks into our adventure the elders offered me a 'skin name,' which meant I would be recognised as family within the Kukatja tribe. I was surprised, elated and humbled, and accepted my new name, Tjapanardi, proudly. (Tjapanardi is a family name, like Smith, but belongs within a clan.) I understand and honour their beliefs, and now have a place within these people's lives as a relative. It meant that Kim became my grandfather.

Some of these men could still remember seeing their first 'white fella' and wondering what made the strange tracks (tyres). Most had been under the influence of our way of life for less than 20 years and practised adeptly all the bush skills of hunting, gathering foods and medicines, tracking, spiritual values, ceremonial duties. They also possessed an uncanny ability for mental telepathy. It was humbling to be in their presence. My apprenticeship in bushcraft skills had begun in earnest and I was taught everything from the difference between beetle and spider tracks to stone tool-making.

The last weeks of our survey required a helicopter, a Jet Ranger, and a pilot hired from Alice Springs, Christine Davies, the only female commercial chopper pilot in Australia at that time.

My first flight in a helicopter was nearly my last. We had just flown over one of the new seismic lines Mobil Oil was working on. I was in the front passenger seat when suddenly every warning light on the dashboard turned red and some started flashing. Christine immediately put the machine into a nosedive from 150 metres, and we hurtled towards earth at 200 kilometres per hour. No need to ask a stupid question, the pilot's concentrated face told it all: the chopper was in trouble and so were we. I can't remember what I thought about, if anything, but my heart was racing and I knew death was a possibility. Just before impact Christine pulled up, flared out and we landed with a thud.

The rotors stopped and we all scrambled out, thanking Chris her for her coolness and control, which meant we were alive and unhurt. After an examination of the stricken beast Chris explained that the battery had overheated and cooked itself. We would not be able to start the machine again and we had no emergency signalling devices or radio power (EPIRBS and satellite phones had not yet been invented).

We were now in a real survival situation in the Great Sandy Desert.

Christine, Kim, Peter, Joe – a very old traditional elder – and I sat in a circle and discussed our options. It boiled down to two choices: stay and wait an unknown length of time because no one knew our location, or walk out.

Considerations:

» The battery was completely dead, therefore no communication with the outside world.
» Possible emergency signals: make an SOS on the ground, smoke and my signal mirror.
» No one at Balgo knew exactly what direction we were going on that day, but they did know it was only a one-day trip, so we'd be missed at mealtime that night – then what?

- » We had limited water – 6 litres – and some cans of soft drink.
- » We had sandwiches for lunch: one meal.
- » No other food rations on board, but enough bush-tucker plants available to curb hunger.
- » My survival kit had two soup stock cubes, a tea bag and coffee sachet.
- » Daytime temperatures averaged 34°C; night-time could be as low as -3°C.
- » No rescue blankets – only fire to keep us warm at night.
- » Balgo was about 100 kilometres away and no roads from it in our direction.
- » Nearest track, the seismic line, was 8–12 kilometres away, but was a big catching feature to walk to.
- » There was a good chance of a manned camp on the northern end of the line.
- » Kim and I had the fitness and ability to walk to the track and return.

The night-time freezing temperature was a big factor in the decision for Kim and me to walk back to the seismic line for help, since we had with us the very old and very fragile Joe. Christine and Peter were both physically in good health.

I spread out my survival kit. We added everything from our pockets and from the chopper that might be useful.

Kim and I took 2 litres of water each, a cigarette lighter, notepaper and pen, mirror, compass and some first-aid supplies (for walking injuries). We consulted the aeronautical large-scale map one more time for main features then headed off on a north-east bearing, aiming high so as not to miss the southern end of the track –

which was a possibility if we walked straight east. We left around noon, walking at about 3 kilometres an hour. We decide to set fire to large dead trees as markers to get back to the chopper on foot or (optimistically) as markers to return with a rescue party. We also made tripods of sticks where 4WD vehicles could easily cross the dry creek beds. I am still proud of those ideas.

At about 4 p.m. we saw a grader moving north, obviously on the seismic line. We desperately ran after it but, just like in the movies, it faded into the distance and our hopes of an early rescue were dashed. I lay on the freshly graded sand and laughed at Kim's colourful description of the unobservant driver. We now knew, however, that the line was still being worked and that the grader was probably heading to a base camp, so rescue was just a matter of time. Kim removed his leather sandals as we started walking on the soft sand, but he'd only taken six steps before I called him back to look at a large desert scorpion, tail up ready to strike. Kim had straddled the venomous creature on the fifth step. Just one more reason for keeping up your safety standards in such situations. With footwear on this time, we had walked for about half an hour when a droning noise drew nearer from the south and a 4WD ute pulled up next to us. It was driven by a young field assistant, who was astonished to see us: 'Where in the bloody hell did you two come from?'

I couldn't resist: I pointed skywards and said, 'Up there, mate'. We explained in detail as he drove us to the base camp, which was about 50 kilometres north. With little fuss the camp manager contacted Father Hevan, the head priest at Balgo and the only person with a phone. We then led a rescue party of 4WD vehicles to our colleagues. Our burning trees and tripods paid off and we returned to a very welcoming committee of three. Back at the seismic base camp we were treated well and the next day flew out from their dirt airstrip in a fixed-wing light aircraft back to Balgo Mission.

Eight days later, accompanied by a new chopper battery, Christine, Kim and I flew back to the seismic camp in a fixed-wing charter plane, borrowed a vehicle and drove back to the chopper. It started and Kim and Christine bravely took off. Left on the ground, I turned back to the lonely borrowed 4WD and noticed that it had two flat tyres. There was only one spare. And they call me 'Lucky Bob'! I pulled off the inside rear vision mirror and signalled to the chopper. They saw the flashes and me indicating to them to return, which they did. I explained my predicament and jumped into the chopper. It was a nerve-racking experience to clamber back inside that so-called flying machine, but we flew effortlessly back to Balgo Mission.

Kim wrote a letter to Mobil Oil in Perth thanking them and gave them a grid reference for their stranded vehicle. It's probably still there. Seven weeks had passed now and I was heading back to Perth with a host of new experiences and a heartfelt compassion for the traditional desert peoples – my new family. When I was asked what I learnt: 'I learnt how much I didn't know'.

# Chapter 4
# HONING MY SURVIVAL SKILLS

## BROOME PEARL DIVER

I was already a very experienced scuba diver and had done some professional salvage jobs in my off-seasons from crayfishing. In 1983, a year after the desert trip, I accepted a job as a pearl diver out of Broome on a boat called *Seeker* with a guy called Feathers. We had the job of arranging the live pearl shells dumped by the drift divers onto the company's licensed 2 hectares of ocean floor 16 kilometres out to sea off the north end of Eighty Mile beach – the middle of nowhere. Our job was to collect all the shells and place them in rows the correct way up or they would become stressed and possibly die.

It was a physically demanding job with anywhere between five and eight hours underwater a day, at a depth of 20 metres in murky brown water. Our air supply was pumped down a hose to each diver from a large petrol-driven compressor (known as a 'hookah') on the boat deck. We had an hour underwater then an hour up on deck during daylight until we had completed our tasks. We worked alone; that meant no one was on the boat: the hookah pumped all by itself. We are talking about working in tropical waters with the accompanying sharks and highly venomous sea snakes. The sea snakes aren't aggressive but the bastards are very inquisitive! Molesting a lone diver appears to be their idea of fun: 'Let's tap on the edge of his face mask! No, let's suddenly appear between his arms! Or (even better) let's wrap around the hosepipe leading to his mouthpiece and watch him have a fit!' I had only one hour of diving when I did *not* see a sea snake. The small, medium and large tiger and/or hammerhead sharks I saw regularly.

It was four and a half months of hard work. The most dramatic bad experience was when the lonesome compressor stopped at the end of a five-hour underwater day. Feathers and I had to do a 'free ascent' from 20 metres. You have to rise slower than an air bubble would, without panicking. As you rise, you need to expel any air that may be expanding in your lungs; otherwise you will rupture your lungs and possibly die. This was the second time the compressor had stopped for no apparent reason – dangerous stuff. I ascended slowly enough as not to damage my lungs, but I got a nitrogen bubble stuck in my left wrist joint (which I had sprained earlier that day) and contracted 'the bends' – a diver's nightmare. An air bubble stuck in a joint causes excruciating pain, bending you in agony – hence the nickname. I had two choices: take a ten-hour sail back to Broome, then a two-hour flight with the Royal Flying Doctor Service (RFDS) to the Fremantle barometric chamber, or go back to the bottom in the pitch-black night. The longer I waited, the worse the pain and the greater the possibility that the bubble could shift into my spine, or worse, my brain – then I'd be dead.

My choice was to dive down deeper than my last dive (20 metres) and ascend *really* slowly, causing the air bubble to shrink and be dissolved back into my bloodstream, eventually to be exhaled as a gas. We sailed 4 nautical miles to our sister ship carrying the drift divers. With their moral support I started the descent at around 8.30 p.m. to a depth of 85 feet, or 25 metres. Feathers came with me and when I reached the bottom the pain had completely gone. It was 'dark as goat's guts' and a place to be afraid of, as sharks and giant gropers feed at night, and they are plentiful. Fist over fist along the thick rope of the shot line (a heavy weight holding it tight) was my tedious rate of ascent. About thirty minutes later we arrived at a tag indicating we were 25 feet or 7.5 metres beneath the boat, where I need to stay for 15 minutes to aid my decompression. (This had been calculated for me earlier from medical US navy dive tables.) Feathers patted me on the head, and as prearranged departed to the safety of the vessel above. Each second seemed to take a minute and believe me, I prayed to God Almighty to let me live through this. I was terrified – several times the large dark shapes of sharks passed, leaving swirls of phosphorus from their tail strokes. I had a dive torch but could not bear to turn it on in case that triggered a shark attack. I looked up at the eerie silhouette of the rope leading to the triangle of the hull, and the dim glow from the deck lights created a ghostlike scene. My eyes were closed and my hands clasped as I prayed, 'Dear God, please let me live'.

At the exact moment my luminous watch hit the 15-minute mark, I started up fist over fist once more. My movements were slow and deliberate, keeping my fins still and breathing very deeply. I could feel and hear my heart pounding inside my wetsuit as I crept closer to the hull of the boat. Finally I heaved myself up the ladder, dropped my face mask onto the deck, and just sat on the engine hatch with my head in my hands, just thanking God. All the other divers understood I needed time alone as many of them had experienced the bends themselves. No-one spoke until I finally said 'Thank God that's over' and from them I received words of understanding.

The pearling season finished in December and so did I. Never again – and I hope that no one else in the world has to ever endure that pain and fear just to make someone rich.

## Testing my survival kit

By 1984 I had resigned from SABRE and had registered my own company, Bob Cooper Outdoor Education. At that time I designed a mini survival kit that literally fitted into a plastic soap container. It was lightweight and small enough to be carried in my shirt pocket yet had the essentials to keep me alive. This meant I was more likely to carry it with me everywhere I went, no matter what form of transport I chose – land, sea or air. It provided me with what I *needed*, not what I wanted. What I *wanted* would fill a suitcase and that, like many survival kits at the time, was too large to be convenient and therefore was sometimes left behind. Sadly, that is exactly what happened with several people who perished in the outback

– their gear was still in their vehicle or base camp and not on them when they needed it.

How could I prove the worth of my mini survival kit?

I decided to walk solo, unaided and with no backup for 162 kilometres through the Pilbara region in Western Australia with only the prototype kit. No food, no sleeping gear; just my clothes, the kit, maps and 2 litres of water in a plastic bag to start my journey. Obviously, I survived. But not without incident, starting with the unusually high temperatures for October – most days were a sunny 44°C.

Day 1: after being dropped off at the starting point by good friend Ian Lancaster, I earnestly prayed for a safe journey. My first task was to navigate to a blue dot on my map, a waterhole 14 kilometres away. I was nearly there and following a dry creek bed leading into my target when I came face to face with a scrub bull. Weighing in at about 1000 kilograms of muscle, they will take on anything that dares enter their territory, including vehicles. The bull had been lying down about 15 metres away, but now erupted up angrily and started thumping the ground with its front hooves, creating a mini dust storm. It was raising and lowering its head, bellowing and blowing large bubbles of dust-covered snot, an unsavoury representation of a bovine. With a great lack of knowledge in the art of bull fighting I tried my best to scare this Uluru-sized thing with horns by yelling and waving my arms and also kicking dirt in the air – I now know you don't do that!

Its response was to bellow even louder and start pawing the ground alternately with its front hooves, obviously getting ready to charge. When it lowered its horned head to bellow and snort, I took my leave. I ran to save my life to the nearest stand of trees, about 30 metres away, and that triggered its attack. Snot and all, it started a thundering full charge after me. I beat it to the tree by about three seconds and up I went like a scared rat, then thud! The bastard rammed the tree but Koala Bob was not moved. I was glued to the highest, strongest branch that would support my trembling frame. Again it head-butted the tree then looked up, with very little compassion in its eyes, and bellowed at me as if to say, 'Come on down and fight!' Bugger that. My hero status was severely dented but I was alive, and I was staying that way. After 38 minutes it huffed off. I slid down the white bark of my most favourite tree in the world and was off like a rocket in a crouching run to freedom.

At my first destination, a pretty waterhole at the top of the ranges and the entrance to a spectacular gorge, I rested, purified some fresh water, consulted my map and confidently headed into the gorge.

Unbeknown to me, it was the entrance to another life-threatening situation that I could never have predicted. It was still day 1 and late afternoon, the temperature was dropping and there was a cooling effect from a light easterly breeze. I was admiring the beautiful reds and browns of the banded ironstone layers that form the 80-metre-high gorge walls. Looking up meant I wasn't looking down. Then some movement caught my eye and I glanced down, then forward – and stopped dead. I was standing in front of a pack of dingoes that were ripping and tugging apart a small, freshly killed kangaroo. I was surprised how close I was to them, but my initial fascination turned to fear when the alpha male took a particular dislike to me approaching their meal. With a deep, low growl his hackles rose and his lips rolled completely back, exposing clenched teeth. Dribbling copious amounts of blood-coloured saliva from his lower jaw and with slow but deliberate, angry steps he approached me head-on, one snarling step at a time, now fewer than 10 metres from me.

The others darted behind me and formed a semicircle blocking my retreat, indicating that they were about to attack as well. I locked eyes with the leader and tried to stare him down, but with no effect. Five metres now separated us. I squatted down, with our eyes still locked, I felt around with my right hand for something I could use. Sand, more sand, then at last I gripped a rock the size of my hand – I had a weapon. Slowly I stood up and while I was off-balance he made his move. He ran, then as he sprang I smashed the rock onto the top of his skull. He hit the ground on his side, but got to his feet immediately. Groggily he ran away from me and fell down whining and shaking his no doubt fractured skull. Without delay the other five joined him and milled around the wounded male, which was still whining.

I retreated backwards and away from their kill, rock in hand poised for any attack, eyes fixed on the pack. Once out of sight I jogged, as the light was fading, until I came upon a deep billabong. Here I built a large fire on the water's edge and made five fire torches out of dead grass, bound onto sticks with thin vine runners. These were to light in defence of a possible revenge pack attack in the night. I could also escape into waist-deep water and easily defend myself there. That night I lay wide awake in anticipation as the hours of total darkness moved at a snail's pace until first light, but nothing happened – except I got little sleep.

The next day I covered 42 kilometres without any more hair-raising experiences. In the following quieter five days I used the kit contents to purify all my water and the compass to navigate, took care of minor first-aid problems and used fire for many things, including cooking a spangled perch I'd caught (two large ones make a substantial meal). I celebrated my achievements day by day with a slice of stock cube made into a soup mixed with Mineritchie wattle seeds, which added a garlic flavour, or my favourite dish, spangled perch and bulrush stems – adding a hint of chicken stock makes a fabulous soup. I had found an old beer can at a windmill, which I modified to make the soup in and use as a cup.

The plastic bags I used to successfully carry water over long distances were made by sliding the water-laden bag inside one sleeve of my jacket with the remainder wrapped around for protection, and the other sleeve as a shoulder strap. An excellent way to carry water, which I needed when travelling between waterholes and windmills that were marked on my map. I always carried a little more than I thought I required, just in case that water source was dry and I had to reroute or travel back. I cannot overemphasise the importance of having enough water and playing it safe with the amounts you carry and consume. Using that old beer can I had found, I was able to measure accurately how much water I drank each day, the most being 11 litres, the least 7 litres per day.

Day 5 was bloody hot and I remember following a dry river bed into a beautiful waterhole, but I was just too tired and too hot to bother fishing. I washed all my clothes and socks and just floated like a log in the shaded, shallow, lukewarm waters. (I never swim alone in deep water; I'll only wade in waist-deep – immersing a hot body in cool water can cause cramps. In shallow water I cannot drown.) Wattle seeds boiled in my tin can and another brew from my fading tea bag was all I needed as I lay next to the low light of my fire on the soft, warm sand in my million-star accommodation. I pondered my past and future with an honest and modest sense of accomplishment, for I thought that by the following night my kit and I could successfully complete this test.

On day 6 at sunset with high spirits and in good physical condition (even though I'd lost 8 kilograms) I arrived at my finishing point, the Sherlock Station homestead, to a very warm welcome from the then owners, Caroline and Bruce May. The kit had proved its merit and I had also learnt what should be added to or subtracted from it. I also learnt a tremendous amount about myself on that journey and it was the impetus for me to offer an advanced course through that same area. This allowed me to watch other people as they too grew both in knowledge and character. That first walk was the birth of what is now my signature Mark-III survival kit, with 34 useful and mainly multipurpose items.

## MAYDAY NUMBER TWO

It was in the 1980s that I experienced my second mayday on the ocean. It was on a 20-metre steel prawn trawler in the Exmouth Gulf. The gulf was an extremely dark, lonely place at 2 a.m., but the water was calm. I was a guest on board, collecting venomous sea creatures for my ongoing survival research. The boat caught fire and we were taking in water due to a melted exhaust outlet seal on the stern of the vessel. The skipper, Garry Flinn, displayed exceptional self-control as one problem after another presented itself. First the engine room was on fire. With the nets still down, we needed to keep the motor running to winch them up. Next the motor was overheating, as the engine's water pump had stopped, and could seize if over-revved. Slowly we pulled up one net at a time because both together could cause the boat to capsize. Then the electric bilge pumps stopped pumping: fire had now spread to the aft storage section. We needed to free up the life raft on the wheelhouse roof, one deckie was starting to panic, the manual bilge pump wasn't keeping up with the water intake and the boat was now wallowing. Once negative buoyancy is reached, a steel trawler will sink within three minutes.

With the last puff of the last fire extinguisher we put out the fires then blocked the leak with bed sheets. We were rescued by another trawler and, as Garry predicted, under towing, the water in our boat rushed forward, lifting the stern up enough to stop the leak completely and allowing safe towage back to Learmonth anchorage. Garry's experience, rehearsed emergency procedures and common sense saved the boat and possibly our lives. Taking to a shallow-sided, flat life raft in shark-infested waters was not an appealing prospect. Sharks were circling, waiting for their ritual feeding frenzy to start. They had been trained by the prawn trawlers' habit of throwing non-saleable fish and crabs back over the side. You could see them in the deck lights, and if the boat had sunk we would have been part of that menu. I can't overstate the control Garry had in this life-threatening situation. Everything he said and did was thought out before being verbalised, and each move took us one small step closer to resolving the main problem.

# BYO SHARKS

In 1993 my third ocean disaster loomed upon me, again on a professional fishing boat, this time out from the isolated town of Port Hedland with an old mate, Munro. I went out for a day's relaxation before I was due to lead a 200-kilometre survival walk through the adjacent Chichester Ranges. With me was Nigel Thomas, an assistant survival instructor. We were on our way to shore after pulling in Munro's 500-metre net, full of large mullet and a couple of very lively two-metre-long bronze whaler sharks. We got an extra-large swell up our backside that made all the gear, and me, slide down to the front of the punt. It nosedived, end for end, capsizing instantly. One moment, all good – next moment fighting for my life. I sank, together with the net – and two sharks fighting for their freedom. My nightmare was being permanently entangled in this netting. I was pushing it away from me and trying to prevent the mesh from hooking itself onto the buttons of my shirt as the net and I sank slowly. The sharks didn't help as they swam portions of the net across and around my body – my pearl diving days' experience kicked in and my fears did not develop into panic. I actually used the nets' resistance to push myself upwards, but not too fast, in order to conserve oxygen. Finally I reached the surface, gasping in lungfuls of fresh air, still with heaps of netting around, but now able to breathe. The net had reached the bottom and the down drag had stopped. Ironically my bush hat popped up in the tangled net right next to me, as if to say 'save me too!' so I grabbed it and plonked it unceremoniously on my head, and watched the rest of the wet evening disappear in the murky depths below me. Munro and Nigel were already clinging onto the upturned hull. I swam over and latched onto the side of the boat. All three of us were shaken but with no injuries. I'm still proud of those guys for the calmness and humbled by the concern they showed for my wellbeing. We discussed the possibility of a dash swim to the shore, 2 kilometres away, but the 6-metre tide was still going out and to swim against that was dangerous. The sun was going down and our unanimous decision was to stay with the boat all night and hopefully drift in close to the shore the next day. No one mentioned sharks but we all had that unspoken fear. We were now in tiger-shark-infested waters and night-time is their feeding time. My legs felt like bait dangling down. I tried to keep them up under the hull but that angle was impossible to maintain without lots of effort and I knew it would be at least a day before anyone realised we were out there, I knew better than to waste my precious energy.

I privately prayed for help and I am sure both other men 'went there' during one of the periods of total silence. The water was warm, it being the tropics, and with only the slightest of breezes physically we were comfortable. As the sun started to set my shark fears became, let's say, more acute. It had been about three hours and now the beautiful golden-red aura of the sunset wasn't appreciated in our despair.

Just before total darkness we heard the sound of a motor – was it a boat or a plane? There was no way of making it out. Finally a dark shape appeared, a lone fisherman in his runabout, who hauled us into the safety of his boat. He had seen a strange silhouette (the hull and motor leg) while admiring that beautiful sunset and only out of curiosity had come to take a look – we probably owe him our lives. He towed our boat back to shore, then kindly offered to help us recover the lost net and fish, which we did. The sharks were gone.

Nigel and I met the group on time the next day, as planned, and we all successfully completed the ten-day survival walk. With solid earth under my feet I had a much deeper appreciation of the pleasure of just being alive and safe.

# FROM HERO TO ZERO IN ONE WORD

In 1995 Dave Alloway, the chief desert-survival instructor with Texas Parks and Wildlife Service in the USA, contacted me, and we began to exchange ideas and views on teaching desert survival. In '96 I decided to attend one of Dave's three-day courses in Texas, both as a visiting instructor and to contribute and learn when I could.

I landed in Dallas in May. An old mate of mine living in Dallas, Garry Stewart, volunteered to drive me down in his 4WD to the south-east of Texas to the 300,000 acres (109,000 hectares) of Chihuahuan Desert wilderness called Big Bend Ranch State Park. The park extends along the Rio Grande from south-east of Presidio towards Lajitas in Brewster County.

After a 14-hour drive and an overnight camp, we arrived just after noon at the designated east-side entry, a boom gate at the end of a lonely dirt back road. It was a sweltering 38 degrees Celsius with a slight breeze.

But the combination we'd been given did not open the huge lock on the boom gate. No amount of guessing different 4-digit code combos worked. Frustration set in and I realised that nervousness about being late for my first meeting was taking over. Standing there with both hands on my hips I thought: what I would do in Australia in this situation? Drive along the fence looking for another gate or damaged fence for an entry point, of course. I had only to follow this fence line with my eyes to see 200 metres away a saggy section hanging off an old corner straining box. We drove there and, using pliers, untied the wire, drove in and re-tensioned the fence better than we found it – I was in!

Driving slowly along this track I started to appreciate the sheer rugged beauty and strangeness of this new place. This track was grey limestone – nothing like our red dirt but just as dusty. The map showed a distance of 32 kilometres to the ranch house. I felt a bit nervous about being a guest instructor in an extraordinary cactus-laden landscape where the coyotes howl, monster tarantulas crawl, black bears and mountain lions roam freely. Cruising at about 60 kilometres an hour with the windows down, fresh desert air filled me with new and exciting odours which complemented my mood of excitement. We drove over a rise and down into a dip – then had to brake hard to avoid a collision with a car parked smack in the middle of the track. A woman was desperately waving her arms to alert us to the obvious. Both rear tyres were punctured and she only had one spare. She didn't want to drive off the road on the punctured tyres because she thought that would ruin them. Quickly explaining that a short distance will not damage deflated tyres, I got the vehicle off the track out of harm's way and Garry parked ours off-road as well. As she explained her predicament the woman kept saying 'we got' this and 'then we tried' that. 'Who's "we"?' I asked.

'Oh, that's my friend.' A woman in her late fifties had walked off with a half-litre of water to walk for four hours and if she didn't find any help she'd return. An eight-hour walk in 38°C heat with only 500 millilitres of water and no map was suicidal. (They had a map: it was still on the dashboard, overlooked in their panic.)

Fortunately the woman had only been gone 20 minutes, so I sent Garry to fetch her back while I took off the punctured tyres. When Garry and the friend returned, the women gathered their valuables as I loaded on the two flat tyres, and the four of us continued on in Garry's 4WD. We arrived five minutes late for my rendezvous with Dave but were greeted with a very warm reception.

Rescue story explained, the women were taken to a bunkhouse and given a meal and overnight accommodation. Their tyres were repaired and they were now safe and happy. It turned out they were booked onto the next survival course but had come a few days early without notice, thus creating their own survival story. A story which could have ended in tragedy as there was no one else within a day's walking distance of their stranded vehicle and absolutely no water in that quarter of this massive wilderness area.

After dinner I was offered a few beers on the porch with Dave and his survival staff. I had gained hero status by now, having rescued the stranded women and having worked out a way into the Park without using a code.

It was while answering loads of questions about our Australian outback that it happened. In reply to a question I said, 'I thought all you Yanks would have known that'.

There was dead silence. Most of the eight men folded their arms, two put down their stubbies, a couple wearing hand guns leaned forward and stared at me.

'Obviously I've said something wrong?'

No one moved and no one spoke – it was nerve-racking: 'Come on blokes, what did I say to offend you all?'

At last, Dave spoke. 'You called us Yanks. We're not Yanks, we're Southerners.'

'You mean, the civil war – 1861 to 1865?'

'Yes, that's right,' from one of the grumps.

Then my Aussie sense of humour nearly got me shot. 'So you're sore losers – is that it?'

That went down like a lead balloon – and so did my hero status. Two men walked away before I could explain that was a joke and the rest of the world outside the USA believed all Americans were Yanks – there was even a movie with that title. Didn't matter to some of them – 'We're not Yanks!'

The rest of my stay, however, was fantastic, both in learning and sharing, and that started a brother bond between me and Dave Alloway, which is still in my heart, even though he has since passed away. I still miss him, his talent and his generosity.

**OWL WISDOM: Don't panic and leave your vehicle to attempt to walk for help when you have the resources available in your car to keep you alive. Those women had several days' food and water on board. They should also have put up stick signal tripods as a warning to prevent a collision with their stranded vehicle.**

**You can drive slowly for only a very short distance on flat tyres and not ruin them.**

# PART 2
# OUTBACK SURVIVAL

# Chapter 5
# CONTROL

## KNOWLEDGE DISPELS FEAR: THE PSYCHOLOGY OF SURVIVAL

What are your fears? I often suggest that people write down their five biggest fears in life. Then I ask, 'What have you done about them, or are you waiting until they are thrust into your face? How would you cope?' The darker side of fear is panic.

What if two, or more of them, are thrust upon you at once? Such as: *I'm lost, I am alone and I fear death.*

Now we are talking about survival – and survival situations can happen in an instant. Think about this: you've got lost and now bogged and no one knows where you are. It's extremely hot and you have nearly run out of water. Firstly the fears from the emotional half of your brain kick in and kick in hard. Your body will react to the perceived fears as if they are real and, if you don't stop them, these fears will override the other, rational half of your brain and you will start making decisions based on these emotional thoughts.

Uncontrolled fear leads to panic and the only thing that can defuse fear is knowledge. *Knowledge dispels fear* – this is a very old but true saying.

The same applies to a survival situation when you know what to do. The rational side of your brain will calm down those emotions; not stop them, just put them back where they belong: below your rational thinking. Knowing what to do will allow you to create a realistic plan and realistic plans don't usually fail. It is the failure to plan that lets us turn that misfortune into a potentially life-threatening situation which sometimes seems out of our control.

When we experience fear we produce cortisol in our brain, giving us a quicker response time in our decision making, and a burst of adrenaline so we can perform the physical tasks our mind asks us to do. I would like you to learn to keep your fear level under control and use that energy in a survival situation to your advantage. Do not waste it on anything but positive forward steps to resolve the situation or aid your rescue.

## TAKING CONTROL

The only thing you can actually control in your life is your thoughts. That's it – there's the secret. *Control your thoughts if you wish to control your own life.*

Wouldn't it be great if you could take control of an unforeseen situation by being prepared? By putting *thought* into what clothes to wear, the amount and type of emergency kit to take, the amount of water to carry, by leaving the relevant details of your intended walk/ trip with a friend? Of course you know you can control these things – but you have to have *thought* about them in the first place and taken 100 per cent responsibility for yourself.

In a survival situation in the wilderness if you aren't in control, then who is? Mother Nature, that's who. She can be – not cruel – just unforgiving. Keep your thoughts positive and your senses open because Mother Nature will provide everything you *need* today but not everything you *want* today.

## PRACTISE SURVIVAL SKILLS

As I said in the introduction, over the years I have witnessed and felt the fear of death during land, sea and air mishaps where the potential for a fatal outcome was real. Survival skills can replace fear with respect for, and trust in, nature.

I quote from North American Chief Seattle, more than 100 years ago.

*Humankind has not woven the web of life.*
*We are but one thread in it.*
*Whatever we do to the web, we do to ourselves.*
*All things are bound together.*
*All things connect.*

I believe Chief Seattle is talking about respect. It starts with respecting yourself first, and then all other living and non-living things on this earth.

*What you give out is also what you get back.*
*Fight the wild and it will fight you back.*
*Give respect and respect will be given to you.*
*Be in and observe the shifting rhythm of nature.*

Respect for the wilderness dispels the illusions created by fear. Just the right amount of fear is a good thing and can keep you alert, and a sufficient amount of knowledge can keep you positive enough to pull through even a dire situation. If you have practised your knowledge, that is what we call 'experience'. When experience in the subject (in this case wilderness survival) is higher, then your fear level *must* be lower and your chances of survival are even greater.

Even if you have only rehearsed in your mind how you would cope and what you would do in an emergency, it has been proven that your chances of success are at least 10 per cent better than someone who hadn't even thought about 'what if', or employs that cheap insurance policy of 'She'll be right mate'.

 **OWL WISDOM: Fear is a natural emotion and a tremendous force, and if the energy generated by fear can be harnessed and used positively, then fear itself is a great tool. I believe that's why we have it – to protect ourselves by using the fear-driven energy wisely.**

# Chapter 6
# THE BIG 5 PRIORITIES
## – and how to prepare for them

In a survival situation, the first thing to do is to assess your circumstances and what needs to be done. There are five priorities to consider – I call these the Big 5:

> » Water: make, clarify, purify and transport
> » Warmth: fire and windproofing
> » Shelter: rain, cold, windproofing and sun protection
> » Signals: day and night – audible, visual and directional
> » Food: available, foraged, trapped and fished

I believe in the kit I have designed and the contents I am about to share with you. It has proven its worth. I have received great worldwide feedback on its effectiveness in varying climates and situations. I'm especially proud that the military version is in active service overseas with our SF Australian troops in the fight against terrorism. The Mark-III is a good kit – I will never say the best kit in the world because you should add to and change the contents to be appropriate for you and the environment you are about to adventure into. The best kit is the kit you modify or create to suit *you*.

The order in which you address these five necessities will change with each situation, depending on variables such as climatic conditions, what other useful resources you have with you and how many people you may be stranded with. For instance, even if just one person in the group has an emergency kit, this improves your chances of survival dramatically.

# A SURVIVAL KIT FOR THE BIG 5

Survival situations cannot be planned and they are not usually wished for, but they should be expected and prepared for. That is why I design, carry and believe in survival kits.

In reality we need only to consider two simple aspects:

1 Will the contents provide my needs to survive in a wilderness area?
2 Will the contents fit my kit's dimensions?

When designing a kit to carry on your person the main considerations are size and weight. That is, small and light enough for you to take with you everywhere, every time, whether on foot, bike, horseback, dinghy, 4WD, helicopter, etc. The practical size is to fit a large pocket and weigh around 500 grams. As well, a kit should be sturdy and waterproof and air-portable if possible.

'Air-portable' means no matches or cigarette lighters, as these should not be taken in unpressurised planes or helicopters. I believe flint strikers are acceptable as they are not their own source of fuel.

Currently, no survival kit can be included in your carry-on bag on any commercial aircraft, because it would contain too many 'sharps'. But you can pack a kit in your check-in luggage.

# MY RECOMMENDED MEDICAL ADDITIONS

» Antibiotic tablets
» Diarrhoea tablets
» Anti-nausea tablets
» Antihistamine
» Eye/ear ointment
» Any special personal medications

These medical items should be supplied by your doctor or a pharmacist. The personal medications should be prescription strength, tailored to your metabolism. Take the kit to show your doctor/pharmacist what your size limit is and explain the reason for these emergency supplies.

# MY MARK-III SURVIVAL KIT

1. Plastic container – for storage, mixing bowl, cup, for digging
2. Compass – direction finding
3. Flint (with attached striker) – fire lighting
4. Hacksaw blade – striker for flint, cutting metal
5. Cotton pad – first aid, can also be pulled apart for fire-lighting tinder
6. Whistle – signalling
7. Knife – cutting, probing
8. Plastic mirror – signalling, assist with self-first-aid
9. Tweezers – removing splinters, other minor operations
10. Large plastic bags – water procurement, wind/ waterproofing, carrying water, storage, improvised emergency flotation devices
11. Needle – probing, sewing (make sure eye big enough to take fishing line or cord)
12. Fishing line – fishing, binding, sewing, snares in Ziploc bag
13. Fishing hooks – fishing, gaff
14. Brass swivel – stops line twisting
15. Sinkers – line weights, can be polished as a lure
16. Trace wire – fishing trace, binding, snaring, general repairs
17. Stock cubes – soup, alfoil wrapping as fishing lure (note: stock cubes contain MSG)
18. Cord – multi-use

19. Tea bag – warm or cold beverage (note: tea is a diuretic)
20. Coffee – warm or cold beverage (note: coffee is a diuretic)
21. Glucose tablet – sweet energy boost, fire making with Condy's crystals
22. Purifying tablets – sterilise water
23. Condy's crystals – antiseptic, antifungal, fire making
24. Plasters – for covering small cuts and abrasions
25. Scalpel blade – probing for splinters, delicate cutting
26. Sewing kit – sewing and repairs
27. Alcohol swabs – sterilising/cleaning skin wounds, fire tinder
28. Antiseptic wipes – first aid; contains iodine
29. Magnifying lens – reading, assist viewing in first aid, fire lighting
30. Torch (and separate long-life battery) – light and signalling
31. Multi tool – pliers and multi-uses
32. Playing cards – combat boredom, survival hints
33. Pencil – writing, graphite lubricant, shaved wood as fuel
34. Instruction sheet – memory aid, notes, emergency fuel

The dimensions of the Mark-III are 13 x 8 x 5 centimetres, with room for my recommended medical items and any personal additions.

# SURVIVAL FISHING TACKLE

The line is approximately 15 metres long with a breaking strain of 7 kilograms. There are a variety of hook sizes and colours for different fish types. I suggest using 'blood knots' for your hook, swivel and sinker attachments. Natural baits to look out for include insects, worms, grubs, pieces of animal carcass and feathers. Or look to your kit for inspiration.

Lures that can be made from the kit include:

» The red plastic strip off a Ziploc bag or the alfoil wrapper from the stock cube can be wrapped onto the hook shank
» Moth and insect shapes can be made from the water-purifying wrappers
» Lead sinkers can be scraped to polish as a lure

Using your tackle:

» Experiment with combinations of baits, lures and hook sizes
» Try fishing at different times of the day and night
» Leave your line in as a 'sleeper line' if possible (only in a survival situation)
» Never eat fish that puff themselves up
» Never eat any fish or shellfish if you are uncertain of their edibility

# CONDY'S CRYSTALS – THE MULTIPURPOSE COMPOUND

Condy's crystals, or potassium permanganate, is a purple compound created by London chemist Henry Condy in the 1860s.

Condy's dissolves easily in cold or warm water. Once dissolved into solution, it is widely used as a broad-spectrum disinfectant in a variety of applications, including to irrigate wounds, as a water purifier, as an antifungal and as a topical antiseptic. The strength of this marvellous medication is governed by the amount of crystals you place in solution – the darker the colour in solution the stronger its antiseptic power. Use your survival-kit box as a mixing bowl.

## Water purifier

It takes only five tiny crystals to give a slight pink tinge to the water. Then shake and wait 30 minutes before drinking. I would suggest Condy's only as a backup water purifier because there is no recent research on its effectiveness against *Giardia lamblia* or other waterborne pathogens, but it was used for many years as a water-supply purifying agent and is very effective. Many people on my survival courses (including a surgeon) prefer it as a water steriliser as it is more palatable than the chlorine- or iodine-based alternatives and arguably as effective. If you can boil water for one minute that is the best water purifier.

## Antifungal treatment

Condy's in solution can kill ringworm or tinea. Soak your feet in a bath of dark-pink solution every day for seven days – remember to wash your socks in boiling water after use to kill the fungal spores of tinea.

## Signals

In snow or on wet, light-coloured beach or river sand you can produce ground to air signals and/or direction of travel arrows by using a sprinkling of Condy's crystals to form those shapes.

## Fire lighting

Mix half a crushed glucose tablet with the same amount of Condy's crystals and then, using the side of the knife blade, scrape the two together on a hard, dry surface. The mixture will spark and flame. Be ready to place dry, finely shredded tinder on the brief flame.

I have also used a pale-pink solution as an effective mouthwash for a gum infection and two cups of pale-pink solution helped cure an upset stomach.

*Note:* If you use Condy's crystals in solution on your skin it will dye your skin a purple/brown colour which washes off in a few days. It has been reported that some people have had skin irritations from repeated use of Condys solution; in 30 years of using it with scores of people I have never seen the slightest adverse reaction on anyone.

I include Condy's crystals as my first choice for an antiseptic/antifungal treatment in my personal survival kit.

## PLAY YOUR CARDS RIGHT

In 2007 I was handed a small deck of playing cards by a friend, Saskia Clark, who'd attended several survival courses with me. She suggested I include them in my Mark-III survival kit. They fitted. I thought that playing cards when stranded would be a great occupier of time and mind. Having spent eight days at a windmill, two days stranded on a wet track in the outback and many hours just waiting for people to pick me up in remote locations, I knew these cards would be very beneficial. Then the thought came: could I create a set of cards that would double as a teaching aid?

Each suit is associated with at least one of the Big 5 priorities for survival – hence the words on the pack, 'Play Your Cards Right to Survive'.

- ♠ Spades are all about water
- ♥ Hearts are about warmth and shelter
- ♦ Diamonds are about signals
- ♣ Clubs are about food

## OTHER GOOD SURVIVAL KIT ADDITIONS

Some people wrap fine cord and extra fishing line around the entire outside of their kits, then seal with tape. Bob Hunter, one of the best survival instructors in Australia, includes a photo of his family in his kit. Another survival/ climbing guru, Greg Winter, shakes in two handfuls of fine rice: filling up all the air spaces in his kit, which provides a substantial single meal.

## CONDOMS IN KITS?

Most people believe a condom is a good extra water carrier; however, in my opinion this is not so – they are too delicate to use to carry precious water. They will explode with the slightest jab from anything remotely sharp and – boom! – you've lost your condom and your water. I once watched 20 soldiers try to carry water in them wrapped in cloth, and the furthest anyone travelled was 2.2 kilometres – not good enough for a survival reserve of water. Use your plastic bags for water transport. Condoms in military kits are for waterproofing and concealing small items, or worn by men to prevent urinary parasites entering when wading through tropical swamps.

## GET FAMILIAR

Don't let the first time you use the contents of your homemade or commercial kit be in a real survival situation. Practise and demonstrate how these items work to your family or friends. It is in your best interest that you know the kit does what you believe it can do. Don't live on hope – remember, knowledge dispels fear.

# Chapter 7
# DREADED DEHYDRATION

A large percentage of our body is water, therefore water is what we require to function perfectly. A well-maintained machine produces the best outcomes. For optimum function, we require a minimum of 1 litre per 25 kilograms of body weight per day. We constantly lose moisture through normal daily bodily functions, including 800 millilitres of water vapour lost per day by exhaling. Every drop of water lost must be replaced to prevent dehydration.

We are so dependent on water for a healthy body and mind that a body fluid reduction of only 1 per cent will start to impair our body's thermoregulation system and dehydration will kick in. The loss of just 2–3 per cent of body fluid means you are acutely dehydrated, but even this does not stimulate your thirst sensation. When you are thirsty you are already more than 3 per cent dehydrated. As our fluid levels decrease, so too does our ability to perform tasks and to think clearly. The loss of 2 litres of body fluid through sweat and respiration will reduce your ability to make rational decisions by as much as 25 per cent. If you keep on losing fluid and not replacing it you will end up suffering from what is known as 'dehydration dementia'.

Dehydration dementia has claimed the lives of many people in wilderness areas when they have become lost or stranded with limited water.

## DRINK, DON'T SIP

Some have died from dehydration with water still in their water bottle. Why?

Because when they were nearly out of water they started sipping on their dwindling supply, trying to make it last longer, but *sipping does not prevent dehydration*. When you sip water, first that small amount will be engaged with food digestion in your stomach, then your kidneys and liver will rob the remaining millilitres, leaving absolutely none for your brain to absorb and use to function properly.

In my opinion, the practice of sipping water must be the biggest single cause of dehydration in our great outdoors. The water in your stomach is always better for you than the water in your bottle. You should drink water at a rate of at least one full standard cup (250 millilitres) each time you drink. In other words, instead of taking 200 small sips from a two-litre supply, I suggest drinking that 2 litres in eight good cupfuls. (You may sip the cupful, but consume it in the same amount of time you would take to drink a cup of coffee.) That way a *useful amount* will enter your system, allowing you to stay hydrated and functioning well. Of course, if you need more, drink more.

## OUTPUT VS INPUT

No matter what your size, age, shape or fitness level, an adult should urinate at least 1 litre of semi-clear fluid per day. When the colour of your urine gets darker, or worse, you lose the desire to urinate, you are dehydrated and you need to drink more. Once again, drink cupfuls, not sips. In a survival situation, make sure your companions are checking their urine output and if necessary use your hydrated frequency as a comparison.

## WHAT HAPPENS WHEN YOU'RE DEHYDRATED?

I hope you never get down to your last drop, because I have gone without water for just over three days and it is terrifying and painful. The first symptoms are thirst, then headache, then nausea – similar to a severe hangover.

When you are dehydrated, your kidneys retain as much fluid (water) as possible. Your last passing of urine will be a concentrated orange-brown colour and then you will cease urinating altogether. Then the very worst symptom moves in: you stop sweating. Your body does this to preserve its organs, which are now causing the accompanying kidney pains. Your headache is getting worse and your ability to think rationally is now halved. You are starting to make silly decisions based on your emotional fears. They are starting to take over the rational side of your brain, and each error you make now could change your situation into a fatal one.

Our bodies have about 3 million sweat pores. Each droplet of sweat evaporates, cooling the blood, which is deliberately pumped to just under the skin. The blood returns, cooled, to the body's core. No sweat – no cooling. This causes your blood temperature to rise and is termed 'heat exhaustion'.

How quickly can this happen? In the BBC documentary series *Extremes* I conducted the 'Heat' episode. The presenter was Ken Bradshaw, an extreme big-wave rider. We placed Ken on an exercise bike in a heat chamber in a university in New South Wales to simulate walking in 40°C heat in the desert. Over 90 minutes, Ken was weighed every ten minutes for fluid loss and his core temperature was monitored for heat exhaustion. He lost an incredible 1 litre every 30 minutes – 3 litres in total. He was extremely dehydrated and his skill levels had dropped to the point where he could barely manage simple calculations and moving around became difficult and painful.

To prevent this happening we must consume enough water to replace every drop at the rate we are losing it. Start hydrated, drink while you walk/work/play, then drink more when you have finished. If you have a limited water supply, manage your activity levels so that you don't sweat as much, thus balancing your water loss with your water intake.

From conducting advanced survival courses for more than 25 years in Australia's hotter months, I have observed that we only require *half* the amount of water to perform a physical chore if we conduct that task at night-time. That's what all the other animals out there in hot climates do – let your observations of them be your teacher.

## Symptoms of dehydration

» Thirst, followed by headache, then nausea and vomiting
» Urine: decreased amount and darker colour, then ceases
» Muscle cramps and/or lightheaded when standing
» Tingling sensation in fingertips, toes and lips
» In severe cases: collapse, coma, organ failure

Once you start to heat up internally from heat exhaustion this, untreated, could lead to heat stroke, a very dangerous and potentially fatal disorder. We are only talking about a 4°C rise in your core blood temperature, which causes part of your brain to literally fuse or melt, causing death in 70 per cent of cases.

Your thermoregulation (the way your body regulates your temperature) is affected by:

» Vomiting
» Lack of sleep
» Diarrhoea
» Menstruation
» Excessive workload
» Hunger from missed meals
» Sunburn or excessive burns
» Recent long-distance air travel
» Taking prescription medications
» High sugar levels in diabetics
» Sipping or not consuming enough water

### Treatment for dehydration

» The treatment for dehydration is shade, rest and
frequent small amounts of fluids. Glucose can be added,
as can electrolytes in the form of sports drinks or the
correct powdered mixtures. Some good electrolyte
supplements are now available in effervescent tablet
form. These now have a pleasant flavour, encouraging
the dehydrated person to drink more.

Full recovery from even mild dehydration may take
many hours. During this time it is important to keep the
person resting in the shade, and to keep them drinking
regularly. Remember that they may not feel like drinking
due to nausea, but they must.

## SYMPTOMS OF HEAT EXHAUSTION AND HEAT STROKE

» A person can be sweating profusely if hydrated
» Sweating ceases, then skin can become red, hot, flushed
or blotched
» Skin feels sticky or dry to touch
» Fatigue or weakness
» Muscle cramps
» Strange behaviour
» Headache
» Nausea and/or vomiting
» Dizziness
» Vagueness
» They can also feel cold and start to shiver
» Collapse and convulsions

## Treatment for heat exhaustion and heat stroke

This is a very serious situation. If you don't cool someone with these symptoms down there is a chance of permanent organ damage.

» As for dehydration, they need shade, rest and intake of fluids

» Lie the person down, but keep them off hot ground by using green leafy branches or daypacks as an insulation mat

» If they have on heavy-gauge clothing, undress to underwear

» Quickly moisten their skin and clothing, ideally with a spray bottle or moist cloth, then fan their body to imitate the cooling, evaporative effect of sweating

» If you have ice packs, place them under armpits and groin – this cools the blood

» It is very hard to discriminate between severe heat exhaustion and heat stroke, so all casualties should be immediately evacuated to the nearest hospital, with the evaporative cooling therapy constantly maintained en route. This is a medical emergency.

**WARNING: Do not immerse a victim of heat exhaustion or heat stroke in cold water, as the surface blood vessels will constrict, reducing blood flow to the skin. The effect will be a rise in the core temperature, making things worse. You could kill someone by doing this.**

# HYPONATREMIA

I'm often asked 'Can we drink too much water?' Under certain circumstances, the answer is yes – if the water being consumed is pure (nutrient-deficient) and in large enough quantity, for example, if undertaking strenuous or long-duration exercise such as marathon runs or long endurance walks. In these cases, drinking copious amounts of exclusively pure water is not the best or safest option.

While a considerable amount of water is lost through these sorts of activities, replacement with only pure water can lead to a chemical imbalance in the body's electrolytes and a deficiency in some essential nutrients, such as potassium, calcium, phosphate and chloride. But the main concern is loss of sodium. The lack of sodium in your body is known as hyponatremia and this condition can – and has – led to organ failure.

Hyponatremia can only result from drinking excessive amounts of only pure water. The symptoms of this condition can mimic dehydration, so in these cases giving water without electrolytes can worsen the stricken athlete, worker or hiker. I recommend always carrying electrolyte effervescent tablets in remote areas because electrolytes won't harm a person who is suffering from dehydration, heat exhaustion or hyponatremia, and indeed can be greatly beneficial in all three conditions.

In all these heat-based medical conditions, does the saying 'Prevention is better than cure' sound reasonable to you? Does to me.

# PLAN TO STAY HYDRATED

These are the steps and protocols I adopt for keeping myself and others well hydrated when bushwalking. People become ill when even mildly dehydrated – prevention is far, far better than cure. You can also adopt and adapt these strategies to suit you, your family or colleagues on any outing.

Prior to walking I always educate fellow walkers about the reasons for drinking water and not sipping.

I encourage walkers to wear loose-fitting, natural-fibre clothing that is light in colour and fabric. A scarf or head sock, long trousers and long-sleeved shirt, brimmed hat and sunglasses are all essential, as is sunscreen and lip balm, which should already have been applied. During hot or humid conditions neck scarves can be wetted – the evaporation causes cooling, with pleasant and beneficial effect, and cools the blood in the carotid arteries, which lead to the brain.

Start hydrated. I ask walkers to drink a minimum of two standard cups (500 millilitres) of water before setting off, then top up their water bottles before departure.

When planning what emergency rations to take, I avoid food that requires a lot of water to aid digestion, such as cake, biscuits, bread, jerky, etc. Instead I focus on foodstuffs with a high liquid content, such as soups and tinned stews. On hot days I supply watermelon, oranges and other water-laden fruits at morning and afternoon breaks. It all tops up your fluid level and that's a good thing.

To reduce the possibility of someone suffering from dehydration, I have compulsory rest/drink stops every 40 minutes. During that break I ensure each person consumes water and rests for ten minutes. I call it my

40/10 walking plan. This also decreases the likelihood of muscle fatigue, and gives people the opportunity to treat any 'hot spots' on their feet before a blister develops. The 40/10 plan can be adjusted to suit people's needs.

 **OWL WISDOM: Water is medicine for your brain – stay hydrated.**

# Chapter 8
# FINDING WATER

As I have explained previously, the importance of water management to avoid dehydration cannot be overemphasised. At all times we need to be 100 per cent hydrated to maintain a healthy body and mind. You can manage your water by ensuring that you carry enough with you and use it wisely – but in a survival situation you might have to rely on natural sources. Again, knowledge and preparation will help.

## READY-MADE WATER SOURCES

In most survival situations water is usually high on the priority list. Water-procurement techniques do work, but finding a ready-made water source, such as a nearby waterhole or a working windmill, is clearly preferable, so check your map carefully for any such features. You can also use natural indicators to lead you to water – for example moving downhill, looking out for larger trees, and observing bird flight patterns and/or animal tracks.

Apart from the actual water supply at a waterhole, the surrounding area will also provide a diversity of vegetation you can make use of, such as for shelter materials and firewood. Permanent waterholes also attract wildlife and stock animals you can use for food.

# WINDMILLS

Windmills are marked and usually named on all topographical maps. Most have their name painted on the tank, making them a good reference point.

A windmill is sometimes referred to as a wind pump and, while most are driven by wind, some are driven by solar pumps or fuel-driven motors. Common sense and/or some mechanical knowledge may be needed to start these pumps.

## Health, hygiene and etiquette

A windmill pumps lifesaving water from beneath the ground for all visitors to share – not just livestock, but also a host of native animals that have relied on this water source for generations. You should consider a windmill as an 'outback shrine' and treat it with such respect.

At a windmill, never drink the water directly from the trough as it is a haven for nasty microorganisms that exist naturally in the water, plus the cattle dribble and nasal deposits that get left behind after drinking can also be harmful to us. This water can still be purified by boiling or using sterilisation tablets.

The best place for procurement is from the pipe that fills the tank. Do not try to move this pipe: they are usually very old and fragile and you could easily damage it, rendering the windmill useless for watering stock troughs.

The next best collection stragegy is to scoop water directly from the tank. Another collection point can be created by depressing the float in the trough, which makes the water flow from the outlet pipe. Collect it from that downpipe.

Even if the water looks and smells clean it must be sterilised before consumption because the well itself may contain bird droppings or small dead animals which will contaminate it. Once the water is sterilised, sample that water for its quality. Swirl the water around in your mouth and spit it out – water that is fit for stock is too salty for human consumption and swallowing it could cause nausea. If the water is too salty, then distil it or make a solar still to extract the fresh water. In thirty years I have only found two mills too salty to drink.

The following rules apply at all times, even in a survival situation:

> » Leave mills as you find them
> » Don't shift any pipes – they may break
> » Do not swim in the tank
> » Do not use soap at a mill
> » Do not wash clothes at the mill
> » Do not leave rubbish behind
> » Do not leave traces of blood or blood products
> » Do not light a fire at the mill or within 50 metres
> » Be aware of snakes under troughs and around the mill day and night

These rules, if respected, will allow stock and native animals to move freely in and out of the mill and lessen the chances of harm to yourself or others.

If you find a working windmill or are stranded near one, set up a camp close to, but not at, the mill site. Snakes live at all windmills and some cattle, visiting for a drink, can be aggressive to strangers, in particular bulls and females with calves.

You can rest near the mill in a survival situation but do not camp within 50 metres. If you are just visiting the area then camp no closer than 200 metres away.

Station workers check windmills and clean the troughs on a regular basis, usually once a week. In case you're out of sight or asleep when they arrive, leave a note securely on the windmill frame where it will be easily seen, or on a stick tripod that will attract their attention to the note. Place it high enough that animals can't eat it and in a location where stock won't knock it down.

Don't swim in a tank, for two reasons. Firstly, your body oils and excessive water movement can upset the delicate ecosystem existing in the tank. Secondly, most tanks are old, to very old, corrugated iron, so jumping in could create too much pressure at the seams and it could split and/or tear, dragging you through the jagged rusty tin gap – this would not be good.

Soaps, detergents and blood give off strong odours that can be frightening to both native animals and livestock. The fear of these foreign scents may stop the animals from approaching troughs and drinking and has, in the past, caused the death of stock animals. In one case I know of, more than 100 sheep died because of this.

If the tank and troughs are dry, the mill may simply be turned off. Look for the brake lever system on the windmill – that is, a wire running from the tail down to a lever, which will be a metal pipe or iron bar near the base of the windmill. Release this lever and the fan will start turning (providing it is windy). This starts the pumping action.

Do not climb the mill tower and spin the fan in an attempt to gain water. Most are high and narrow and the whole windmill head could suddenly spin 360 degrees with a wind gust, knocking you off your perch.

> **IMPORTANT:** If there is no water pumping and the tank and trough are dry then you can still get water from the bottom of the well itself. Lower a piece of your clothing weighted with rocks in the pockets on some cord or wire. Pull up the cloth quickly, wring it out and repeat the process. This is easy and surprisingly quick.
>
> **NOTE:** The symbol for a windmill on a map is

## WATER EMBLEM

The Australian Aboriginal symbol for a permanent water supply is carved or painted concentric circles. If you look at that for long enough you would realise that the only place in nature you get perfect concentric circles, is on disturbed water, such as when you drop in a stone. If you see these circles painted or etched on a rock or in a cave it usually means a waterhole is close by.

**Aboriginal symbol for water**

# GNAMMA HOLES

These rock depressions, usually with a permanent water supply, may be marked on your map. They are the habitual ancient waterholes of the Aboriginal peoples. Some are covered with a large slab of flat rock to slow down evaporation and keep them cleaner. You can see other flat rocks propped up on a single stone near these Gnamma holes. In the past, some have speculated that these were spare lids but in fact they are a kind of lizard trap. Lizards would make their homes underneath these platforms, making a welcome meal for visiting tribal peoples.

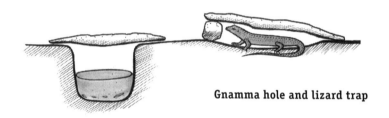

Gnamma hole and lizard trap

# NATURAL INDICATORS OF WATER SOURCES

## Birds

All seed-eating birds must drink daily, usually early morning and late afternoon.

When birds fly to water, their flight path is a direct line and they fly in a tight squadron formation. Flocks of corellas look like a long white ribbon when going to water. Birds flying away from water have a flight formation that is haphazard or more relaxed, and they often stop to forage or roost in trees.

The smaller the bird, the closer their water supply. Finches rarely stray more than 2 kilometres from water. Be aware, however, that flocks of waterbirds overhead could be migrating long distances and may not necessarily lead you to any nearby water source.

## Insects

Observing insects such as mud wasps, European bees and dragonflies can lead you to their water source. They will sometimes guide you to a hollow tree trunk or rock crevice, where you may need to use some ingenuity to access their water supply – for example, using a hollow grass straw or cloth sponge on a stick to access the water.

## Animal tracks

Following the well-worn paths of native and feral animals such as kangaroos, wallabies, cattle, sheep, goats, horses and donkeys will lead you to water. They are all grass-eaters, so need to drink daily.

The main indicators of an active track are fresh dung and paw or hoof prints. Tracks that converge like arrowheads will lead you towards water, but keep in mind that they may split into two different tracks going around an obstruction before rejoining and continuing towards the water source. Bear in mind, too, that tracks lead to and from a water source. If you have found a single trail then save time, energy and sweat by looking for some other water indicators which may give you a clue to start you off in the right direction, observations such as the downhill topography where waterholes usually form, birds' flight paths and flying patterns to and from water, bird calls from a static area, taller and greener trees. Use these observations to start you in the right direction until you find the Y junction of trails which will give you a positive direction.

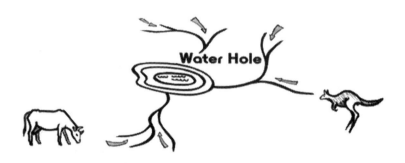

# WATER-PROCUREMENT METHODS

If you can't find a water source now is the time to get clever and use what you have available to make water. There are several methods to use and each has its merit and could be the life-saving skill you need in a real survival situation. So practise these to be competent and confident for when it really could mean the difference between life and death.

## Transpiration method

I have placed the transpiration, or 'bag over a tree branch', method first on the list because it is easy to do – all you need is a plastic bag and some string. Above the simplicity is the fact that of all the techniques using plastic it produces the best results for your effort.

Another positive factor is that it fits into what I believe is the 'energy equation' for survival; that is, one X of effort must yield you two X of return – otherwise it isn't worth expending your precious energy or sweat.

This method works by placing a plastic bag over a tree branch, leaves and all, and making it airtight by sealing it with string. Choose a branch that receives as much direct sunlight as possible. This will create excessive heat on the leaves and the tree will attempt to cool that micro-environment down with moisture vapour. This cooling process, akin to sweating in humans, is called transpiration.

All plants transpire pure water and that's what we are tapping into. Some transpire more than others, with the largest of our eucalyptus species giving off as much as 200 litres per day in water vapour.

The plastic-covered branch sends a distress signal down to the lateral water storage roots of the plant to pump up more moisture to cool it down. The vapour condenses and water is formed. The greatest yield I have witnessed is 900 millilitres from a single bag in one day.

How to use the transpiration method:

» First, select a tree or shrub (the larger or older the tree, the bigger the root system, and the more water will be available from its roots) and check your selection for poison indicators. (See 'The look test', page 124.) In Australia I recommend eucalypts as a first choice as they are easily identified, and to the best of my knowledge all are non-toxic.

» Select a branch that gets as much sun exposure as possible and shake it to remove any loose leaves, seeds, spiders, caterpillars, insects and anything else that might taint the water. (Once when selecting trees for this method we noticed that all the eucalypts in the area had loads of caterpillars on their leaves. I accidently brushed the side of my face against one of them and – zap! – it expelled its stinging juice onto my face, causing a painful burning sensation and some local swelling. That reaction in the back of someone's throat could be deadly and it could happen if mixed with the water produced in your plastic bag. Those caterpillars were only there in springtime but what a great lesson: be observant. We successfully used the local wattle trees instead, which had no caterpillars at that time.)

» Next, look for and remove any leaves that have bird droppings, spider egg cases or mould on them.

» Make sure nearby dead or living branches will not shred your bag if the wind blows them into contact.

» Place the plastic bag over the tree branch. Wrap some toilet paper, cloth or plastic around the branch before you seal up the bag with string. This makes it as airtight as possible, preventing the hot air inside the bag from escaping, and giving you the best yield for your effort.

» Use a clear bag if possible. Black and dark-coloured plastic bags block the sunlight to the branch. The plant thinks it is night-time and reverses photosynthesis, meaning that it does not give off much water vapour, giving a poor yield for your effort. Other colours such as blue, green and yellow do work, but not as effectively as a clear bag.

» The water produced will settle in the lowest corner of the bag. Drain this out by cutting a small hole in the other corner and emptying out the water, then re-seal the hole using string to make the bag as air tight as possible again.

» For the best results, drain the water every four hours; on a hot day you can collect as much as 250 millilitres in the first draining.

» If you can, purify the water before drinking.

## Water from tree roots

Trees store their water in the lateral roots growing just below or on the surface. The more reliable trees are large acacias (wattles), eucalyptus (gum trees), kurrajongs, casuarinas (she-oaks) and the boab. An easily obtainable supply of exposed tree roots can be found in most dry creeks or river beds. Bigger trees have a bigger storage supply, so don't waste your energy digging up sapling roots; they produce very little water.

How to procure water from tree roots:
» Start as close to the tree trunk as possible and dig out the roots, which should be 50–100 millimetres in diameter.
» Cut the root into lengths of 1–2 metres.
» Scrape off about 20 centimetres of bark from around the thicker end.
» Invert the roots into a plastic bag or any sort of 'bucket' – even a clean, deep rock depression – with the shaven, thicker end facing down. Water will seep out.
» As much as a cupful has been recorded from a single 4-metre root.
» It is advisable to purify this water. Purifying all water obtained from the bush is something every survivalist should do to reduce the possibility of health issues.

## Collecting dew

At dawn, a lifesaving amount of water in the form of dew can be collected from a vehicle body's surface and also from sheets of plastic laid out overnight. Your credit card can also 'buy' you some water when used as a scraper. A soft absorbent cloth 'sponge' used to mop up the dew and then wrung out regularly into a container or plastic bag will also help you to survive another day. Dew also forms on some hard, smooth rock surfaces and can form small pools of water.

You can also collect dew from low bushes or moist grassed areas in the early morning by tying your shirt around one ankle and your trousers around the other ankle. Walk through bushes and grasses, allowing the cloth to soak up the water, wringing your clothing out frequently into a container. Again, just to be safe, purify this water before consumption.

## Water from vehicle air conditioners

You can only collect this water if the vehicle engine still works. Run the air conditioner on 'cold' with the fan set on 'high'. Open all the windows to provide the maximum amount of moisture for the air conditioner to process.

Look for the overflow pipe of the air-conditioner condenser under the car (usually located in front of the front passenger's feet) and place a container or plastic bag under it to collect the cool drops of water as they drip down. The water will not need to be purified providing the container is clean. You should be able to gain several litres from a half-tank of fuel – this water is also cold when produced.

Always keep an eye on the temperature gauge to ensure the engine doesn't overheat. If conditions are hot, sit in the car and make the most of the cool microclimate created by the air conditioner while it produces water for you.

If you have not put up the bonnet of the vehicle, do so now; the free flow of air helps to keep the engine cooler. It should be up anyway as part of your signalling plan.

## Solar or desert still

This is an option if you only have a plastic sheet, and is a good way to get drinkable water from salty/brackish water, or from plants:

» Find a suitable area to dig, one that is exposed to maximum sunlight for as long as possible, and dig a hole which is smaller than your plastic sheet but deep enough allow the plastic cover to slope inwards at a 45-degree angle.

» Collect and place as much non-poisonous fleshy plant material or salty/brackish water in the hole as you can. (Poisonous plant vapours can contaminate the water, so do not use anything that resembles something that could even be mildly toxic. See Chapter 13.)

» Place a container in the centre of the hole to catch the falling drops as they form on the ceiling of the plastic and cover the hole with the plastic sheet.

» Push the centre of the cover down towards the centre of the container below and weigh it down in that position using a stone or a few handfuls of sand.

» Peg down the corners of the plastic sheet with small wooden stakes.

» Make the hole airtight by sealing the remaining edges of the plastic sheet with soil.

The sun will heat the moist material inside the sealed hole, causing clean water vapour to form on the underside of the plastic. The droplets will make their way down the 45-degree slope, growing larger and heavier until they finally drop off into your container, and in time you will have enough to drink. For best results, empty your container at the end of the day, and replenish the hole with more fleshy leaves or other moisture-creating substances.

## Solar box

Assess any object for its potential use as a 'box'. A cardboard box lined with plastic, a tool box, Esky, plastic tub – these all make excellent solar boxes. Both solar methods require airtightness, and that the cover is weighted to create a 45-degree angle on the plastic sheet into your clean catching container. Place your plant material or salty water in the box and seal the plastic on all sides of your box with tape of some sort.

The solar box works the same way as a solar still but has a few advantages:

» Saves energy and sweat by not having to dig a hole.
» It is portable, so can be placed in direct sunlight and moved whenever necessary.
» The sides are less likely to collapse inwards and cause sand pollution to the water.

Solar still

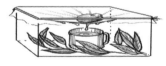

Solar box

Again, in a survival situation, if there is any chance of contamination (such as an unclean container), purify the water before consumption – it's better to be safe than very sorry.

I've used the solar still or box method in every desert survival course I have been involved in (on several continents) but I've never seen one of these produce any more than 600 millilitres of water over a 24-hour period, so you will need several stills for an adequate water supply. In my result for effort equation, nothing beats a clear bag over a tree branch, so take plastic bags, not plastic sheets, in your survival kit. You can always make an airtight bag into a sheet, but not the reverse.

## Ground succulent

*Carbobrotus* is a native Australian succulent commonly called pigface. There are also a couple of introduced species in the same family. It is a creeping, fleshy-leafed plant with daisy-like flowers. You can squeeze lifesaving water from this plant by crushing it in your hands and letting it dribble into your mouth, Kalahari Bushman style, using your thumb on your upper front teeth as a guide for the water flow. You can gain more by wrapping loads of pigface in your shirt, rolling it up tight, crushing it with your foot/ boot and wringing it out, catching the water on a plastic sheet which has a depression in it. The softer yellow/green leaves seem to offer more water and taste less salty. This is what kept me alive for three days on my SAS survival course. The whole plant is edible and the seed pods (when dark red) have a mild, sweet, fig-like taste – enjoy.

## Coastal water sources

On the coastline behind the first line of sand dunes, look for a low depression with a damp, moist area then dig a small round hole with a stick and your hand. Go as

Remote means remote – in the Pilbara region, Western Australia.

Day 8 of the SAS course
(Bob on the left) –
very, very tough, but a
privilege to do it.

Knowledge
– acquired
through good
survival training
– dispels fear.

Drinking water Kalahari style.

This water was produced in five hours – using a plastic bag tied over leaves.

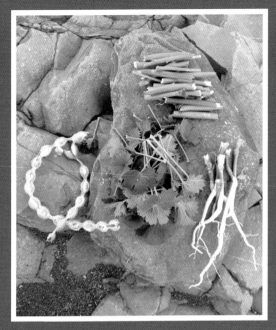

Ingredients for soup
(*from left to right*):
native wattle seeds,
with native celery
and parsnips.

Bush tucker (*from
left to right*): Boab
nut (*top*), yams,
quandong and
sandalwood nuts –
to be eaten raw
or cooked.

Fire made from flint on a cotton pad from the survival kit.

Success! Fire ignited by friction.

It is possible to boil water in a plastic bottle, suspended over a fire.

An effective signal fire at night.

Bob showing direction-finding using a shadow stick.

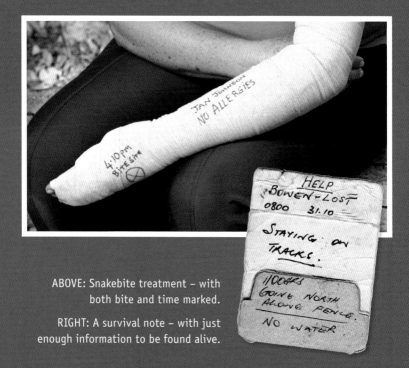

ABOVE: Snakebite treatment – with both bite and time marked.

RIGHT: A survival note – with just enough information to be found alive.

A knife made (by Bob) out of a piece of glass, with a goat fur handle.

Bob demonstrating just how to make signal mirror flashes.

**Mark III Survival Kit**

| | | | | | | | |
|---|---|---|---|---|---|---|---|
| Plastic Container | Cotton Pad | Tweezers | Fishing Hooks | Stock Cubes | Glucose Tablet | Paracetamol Tablets | Pencil |
| Compass - Silva | Whistle | Plastic Bags | Brass Swivel | Cord | Puritabs | Alcohol Swabs | LED Torch |
| Flint | Knife | Needle | Sinkers | Tea Bag | Condy's Crystals | Antiseptic Wipes | Bob cooper Leatherman |
| Hacksaw Blade | Plastic Mirror | Fishing Line | Trace Wire | Coffee | Bandaids | Magnifying Lens | Survival Hints Playing Cards |

Full contents of the Mark III Survival Kit.

Proud attendees of a survival course, Kimberley, 2012.

deep as you can with just your arm. Place long sticks on the walls of the sides to prevent collapse and let the salty water that seeps in settle for a few hours. In that time the fresh water will end up floating on top of the salt water, giving you 2–3 centimetres of fresh, drinkable water. Use a hollow grass straw as a siphon to drink the fresh water.

## Distilling

The only thing that evaporates out of solution is water. So it is possible to turn salty or dirty water into fresh drinkable water. Distilling is the simple process of boiling salty water and channelling the steam through a cooling agent, thus condensing the steam vapour back into pure water. This can be done in a variety of ways, depending on the resources available. The typical 'still' would be a pot boiling on a fierce fire topped by an alfoil cone shape with a plastic hosepipe secured at the apex and made airtight. The hose, which is coiled downwards and run through wet sand or wet cloth, condenses the steam down to collectable water. You can also simply catch the steam by placing an absorbent cloth (for example, a T-shirt) over the pot and squeezing the water out once the steam has condensed into water. Wear gloves and still be careful not to burn your hands because steam is many times hotter than the boiling water.

# CLARIFYING VS PURIFYING

It is just like clarifying a statement – makes it clearer but doesn't change the content. Clarifying water does *not* make it safe to drink. Straining it through your hat, scarf or other material only makes the water clearer by removing suspended matter – and that sometimes makes it more palatable, but nothing more. You must also purify this water before drinking it.

On most of the occasions I have had to filter water, I have only ever needed to use a piece of clothing or hat. There are times when you come across mucky or more naturally polluted water that requires a fine strain. The best improvised filter is charcoal placed underneath a layer of clean sand in the bottom of a shirtsleeve tied off to make a sock shape. The sand catches the larger waterborne particles first. Charcoal is extremely porous and absorbs most if not all other impurities and, most importantly, some pathogens – creating a form of purification, if you have no other means. Several straining sessions through fresh charcoal each time will certainly produce as sterile water as possible for you to consume.

## Gypsy well

This is another way to clarify water. I first witnessed such a well dug by Tjanjanu, an Aboriginal elder, in the Great Sandy Desert. We had arrived at a waterhole that had been mucked up by camels. Tjanjanu simply dug a trench with his hand in the moist soil near the water's edge, let the dirty water filter through the sand, then drank the cleaner water.

I have observed since then that wallabies and kangaroos do something similar, although for a different reason.

Digging a bit further out from the edge allows roos and wallabies to turn their back to the main water supply as they drink from their little gypsy well. This makes them less vulnerable to attacks from behind from their traditional foes – humans, dingoes or wild dogs.

Remember, these gypsy wells only *clarify* water, and do not purify it.

# PURIFICATION

Purifying, or sterilising, water makes it safe to drink. This must be done whenever possible, as waterborne diseases or parasites can cause mild to severe debilitating illnesses which could not only stop you from functioning physically but actually kill you.

In saying that, if you cannot purify your drinking water properly then filter it several times before drinking, as described above – to have and fix an upset stomach means at least you are still alive. Most normal problems, including the common parasite giardia, take several days to develop, by which time you should have been rescued or found your way out.

## Boiling

Boiling water is the most effective way to purify water. Boil vigorously for one minute only. This will kill all dangerous pathogens. Most nasties (including giardia) die between 60–70°C. Water boils at 100°C at sea level and 90°C at altitude. To boil for any longer than a minute would be a waste of valuable fuel and a waste of water, as the evaporation rate of boiling water is massive.

Boiling produces no change in chemical content or taste. You can boil water in a selection of containers including glass bottles, aluminium foil sheets made into pot shapes, bamboo sections, bark dishes and – if you can believe it – plastic drink bottles.

The secret to boiling water in plastic bottles is to start with the bottle full. Tie a wire around the neck and attach to a long stick, like a fishing pole. Dangle the bottle directly over the flames. The water prevents the plastic from melting. The plastic does shrink a little but the container is still reusable.

Red-hot rocks from your fire can be used to boil water in a variety of receptacles. These rocks need to be as hot as possible. Move them by using improvised wooden tongs and place in the improvised water container, such as a bark or alfoil dish, tin container, a concave rock depression or a plastic bag.

Boil water in a plastic bag? Yes. Cut the bag down two sides to make a sheet and line a pre-dug sand hole, depression or cardboard box with the sheeting. Place flat rocks in the bottom of the hole on top of the plastic sheeting (like a tiled floor). Add water, then place the red-hot rocks from your fire directly on top of the rock 'floor' to prevent them melting the plastic and you have done it – boiled water using a plastic bag.

> **IMPORTANT: Water polluted with chemicals cannot be made safe to drink by any purifying method.**

## Chemical purification

You can purify water by using any of the commercial brands of purification tabs available from camping stores – follow the suggested quantities and timings strictly.

Several types contain iodine, so make sure you or anyone likely to consume water purified by this means don't have an allergy to iodine.

Filter pumps and filtered 1-litre bottles are also useful on treks but are too large for personal emergency kits. Size, weight and price are also considerations.

 OWL WISDOM: Look and listen, because very often nature is telling you where water is to be found.

# Chapter 9
# WARMTH

Warmth has two components. One is your choice in preparedness for your day trip or expedition and the other is what the environment dictates to you on the day.

Your choices are what to wear and what you take 'just in case' of a change in the weather or if your plans don't go according to Plan A.

You have more and better options if you wear layers of clothing that you can take off or put on to make yourself as comfortable as possible as the weather changes.

Keeping warm helps to prevent our core body temperature from falling below its low end of 36.5°C. A decrease of only 2°C causes us to develop the symptoms leading to hypothermia.

Hypothermia is a dangerous condition for anyone at any time. Whether on an adventurous trip above the snow line or on a half-day sightseeing walk, nature can and does change its mind and send in the 'wild card' – the unexpected cold-snap. This can happen not only in the obvious cold climates but also in hot desert areas. I have experienced daytime temperatures of 38°C in our central Australian deserts followed by minus 3°C that night.

Take some time to choose the appropriate clobber for outings and take that extra lightweight jacket, raincoat and gloves if you think, or are advised, that you should.

## THE WIND-CHILL FACTOR

If you are stranded in a cold climate, firstly eliminate the wind-chill factor. This is the extra cooling effect that even the slightest breeze can have, because it takes away the precious thin layer of body heat that helps to keep you warm. In the 'Cold' episode of the BBC TV program *Extremes*, presenter Ken Bradshaw was placed in a wind tunnel at 0°C and a breeze of just 10 kilometres per hour was applied. This brought on hypothermia in 30 minutes, one-third of the time of the previous test with no breeze. The stronger the wind speed the greater the wind-chill factor, which means a more immediate need to find or create shelter to reduce rapid body-heat loss.

## WAYS TO KEEP WARM

### Find shelter from the wind

Stay inside your tent or build a shelter. Find a natural rock shelter or cave, dig a trench, use a hollow tree or log, locate natural depressions or furrows in the ground or build a snow cave – do whatever it takes to get out of the wind. Then put on as many layers of clothing as possible and seal all openings, such as sleeve cuffs, trousers and neck area – because it's not the clothing that keeps you warm; it's the thin layers of air heated by your body and trapped between the clothing layers. Your body provides the heat – so trap it and don't lose it. If you continuously lose body heat you will start to shiver to maintain your thermoregulation. Shivering is a vast drain on your body's energy supply. If shivering is not enough, your body will lull into a lethargic mess as you go deeper into hypothermia. All your senses will be dulled, your ability to rationalise will diminish and your cognitive skills will be shot. This combination could be fatal.

## Light a fire

It is still the easiest way to keep warm and, apart from the warmth, fire does so many good things for you (see Chapter 10, Fire). Make sure you always carry some form of fire-lighting and tinder with you on every trip, no matter how short the time or distance.

Heat up rocks about the size of your fist and bury them in the soft sand where you are planning to sleep. These stay very warm for about six hours, and apart from keeping one portion of you warm, it prevents your body heat from being drawn into the cold earth.

Pour boiling water into your water bottles, then wrap in cloth and place in your sleeping bag or inside your jacket for extra warmth. Heated and wrapped smooth, round rocks have the same warming effect.

Construct a reflector wall – designed to reflect the fire's radiated heat. These 'walls' can be constructed from canvas, a rescue blanket, stone, wood or large fallen tree trunks. Put your body between the fire and the reflector wall to enjoy the toasting effect. I have done this on several occasions and found it extremely effective.

Traditional desert people often built two long fires and slept between them for warmth.

## Insulate

Insulate yourself from the cold by creating warm air pockets around your body. Improvise with whatever is at hand: stuff paperbark, dry grass, newspaper sheets, toilet paper or tissues scrunched into balls between the layers of your clothing. Your body will heat up these air pockets and this in turn acts like a crude, but highly effective, form of thermal underwear – a good survival skill.

If you are in a tent or an improvised shelter you can also heat up a confined space by using candles or a gas stove. This simple act may prevent someone from going into a hypothermic state. You must have open air vents to allow some fresh air in. Fuelled stoves/candles will create a carbon monoxide atmosphere which is odourless and can be fatal. To be safe, only burn them for short periods, and never when everyone is resting.

# WHEN FIRE ISN'T POSSIBLE

No fire capability? Get out of the wind and remember to stuff dry filling between the layers of clothing and seal off warm-air escape routes. Wrap something around your head and face. Now you must use your body movement to create heat to keep you warm. Walk if you know where you're going. Walk or jog in circles if you don't want to leave your location. Do stretching exercises, tai chi or dance all night long. Move to keep warm. Don't just sit and shiver – you could die. Catch up on sleep during the warmer daytime.

# HYPOTHERMIA

As I said before, hypothermia can kill, so prevention is paramount.

## Early symptoms

> » The person says they are cold
> » May be confused, display poor coordination and have slurred speech
> » May shiver uncontrollably (*Note:* Shivering may not occur in every case)

If these symptoms are observed, field management and correct treatment are essential as untreated, the person will go into a coma and die.

### *Treatment*

You will need to restore the victim's body heat as soon as possible and get them out of the elements, into a tent or improvised shelter.

---

**DANGEROUS CORE TEMPERATURES AND THEIR EFFECTS**

**36.5° – Lowest 'normal' body core temperature**

**35°C – Hypothermia commences when the core temperature falls to this level**

**34°C – Person is unaware of their condition, shivering, confused; may shed clothing**

**33°C – Person is conscious but incoherent and shivering stops**

**32°C – Person is at serious risk of cardiac arrest**

- » Lie the victim down on an insulated surface above the cold ground – for example, on top of rucksacks.
- » Remove damp or wet clothing.
- » Wrap in dry insulation material (for example, a sleeping bag). Seal the neck area with extra clothing to stop warm air escaping.
- » Heat loss can be a massive 35 per cent from just the head and face area, so cover well, particularly for people with shaved or bald heads.
- » Cover with rescue blanket – reflective side down to reflect back their body heat
- » Give warm drinks – definitely no alcohol.
- » Provide warm air in shelter by lighting camp stoves or candles – remember ventilation.
- » Share body heat of unaffected companions.
- » Apply heat pads, improvised hot-water bottles or heated rocks, all wrapped in cloth, so as to not burn the victim's skin, because at this stage their skin is numbed.

Once the victim recovers, rest for at least 24 hours before moving and reconsider continuing your journey as the victim will be severely weakened.

# STORING ESSENTIAL SUPPLIES OR EQUIPMENT

Cold conditions can affect batteries, liquid medicines and contact lens fluids, and glass jars can freeze or shatter. Use plastic containers where possible and take powdered medicines. Store essential items close to your body to keep them warm.

**COSTS:** Hypothermia must be avoided at all costs! That includes the financial costs when purchasing equipment and clothing – whether for yourself or others.

# RECOMMENDED OUTFIT

My normal outfit and equipment includes:

- » Hat
- » Sunglasses
- » Sunscreen and insect repellent
- » Long-sleeved shirt – not nylon
- » Long trousers – not nylon
- » Jacket – windproof
- » Leather gloves and belt clip
- » Ankle-high boots with quality socks
- » Disposable raincoat
- » Mozzie head net
- » Survival kit
- » Three pressure bandages
- » Rescue blanket
- » Water supply
- » Scarf or head sock

These items greatly improve the chances of survival for me and the people with me.

# Chapter 10
# FIRE

I'm not going to start with 'since the dawn of time' stuff – the barrow I'm going to push is that we require fire to stay alive. But never, ever underestimate the importance of fire. I always rate warmth, signals, cooking and the psychological comfort of a fire as the main reasons I would light one when in a survival situation. A fire does so much more for us physically that it will always be in a survivalist's catalogue of desires in a real survival situation.

We can create fire in scores of ways – by using magnification of heat from sunlight, chemical mixtures, air compression, friction and by electrical means.

Now is the time to caution all you would-be pyromaniacs not to take some of these techniques to the next level and possibly hurt yourselves.

I know this very well myself, having experienced the hospitality of the Royal Perth Hospital's burns ward, the consequence of stupidity in my experimental fire-creation techniques using chemicals.

Only use the simple and safe ways – the true ways of a survivalist.

# REASONS FOR MAKING A FIRE

(In no particular order, since your circumstances will determine what is most important.)

» Psychological comfort – simply feels good
» Warmth
» Daytime smoke signals
» Night-time firelight signals
» Cook food
» Destroy rubbish
» Make charcoal
» Fire-harden wooden tools
» 'Back burn' in a bush fire
» Light to see by (a torch or camp fire)
» Protection from insects and larger animals
» Smoke used in the drying process of meat or fish flesh strips
» Make herbal concoctions for medicines
» Purify water by boiling
» Sterilise bandages in boiling water
» Burn unwanted food scraps that may attract uninvited animals
» Sterilise metal knife blades and needles for first-aid procedures
» Heat some types of rocks before knapping (shaping) into tools
» Bend or straighten wood for tools or traps
» Smoke or flush out animals in hunting
» Burn out areas to sleep on the ground
» Distil salty or unclean water to produce drinking water

# FIRE-MAKING METHODS

## 1. Friction:
» Bow and drill, hand drill, fire thong, fire saw and fire plough
» Metal or stone onto flint rock to create sparks

## 2. Electrical:
You can start a fire using fine steel wool and torch batteries.

First, tease the steel wool out into a strand about the thickness of a pencil. Next, hold one end of the steel wool on the negative terminal and brush the positive terminal with the other end. This will 'arc out', and the 'wool' will glow red hot; this then needs to be applied to fine tinder to achieve a flame.

The heat from the 'arc out' burns the steel wool quickly, so be ready to place this glowing ember into your prepared fine tinder bundle, and blow air (oxygen) into the bundle with your breath, to help to create the flame.

The higher the torch battery voltage the easier it is to burn the steel wool. If you need more power you can tape several batteries together if needed.

Alternatively, you can take the light end off your torch and brush your steel wool across the two different terminal contact points.

## 3. Chemical:
Condy's crystals and sugar mixed and ground together.

Condy's and anything with glycerine in it will also ignite. *Warning:* Be very careful as this can also explode in a confined space and gives off a poisonous gas.

## 4. Pressure:

The first of the two items involved is a piston-like rod with an airtight seal with a small amount of flammable material on one end, and a push-down handle on the other end. The other piece is a hollow cylinder which the piston is driven into by hand with force. The compressed air creates lots of pressure, and this causes the temperature in the bottom of the cylinder to rise to as much as 250 degrees Celsius, and ignites the material on the end of the piston.

Pull it out quickly, and you then have a smouldering glowing ember on the piston end to place into a tinder bundle. Again, blow air onto it to create fire.

Much too difficult for a survivalist to consider in a real situation but I have created a small ember with one made from a solid animal horn and wooden plunger. It took lots of energy from many attempts to accomplish just once.

## 5. Magnification:

>> Through a magnifying lens from survival kit, strong reading glasses, binocular or scope lenses
>> Through water-filled plastic bottles or clear water-filled plastic bags
>> Through a prism of ice
>> Concentrated reflected light from a concave torch/headlight reflector or polished bottom of a soft drink can, or any similar highly reflective concave surface

I have successfully lit fires using all of the above alternative ways except the ice prism (but I've seen footage of this technique being demonstrated, so it can be done).

Just using the fire bow and drill I have in practice or demonstration achieved success more than 500 times on four continents using many types of woods. However, even with that amount of experience I still would not gamble my life, or your life, on that technique alone to save us in a real survival situation.

Life is too precious to gamble with.

So while I endorse the practising of all the alternate ways for fun and experience, I would like you to be fair dinkum about having at least two reliable, safe, 100 per cent proven fire-lighting methods with you at all times when in the wilderness anywhere on earth.

You should also have some respectable tinder. For this I carry a small, flat, rectangular cosmetic cotton wool pad. These cotton pads are cheap as chips and the fluffed up cotton inside is excellent, foolproof tinder.

I prefer a flint and magnesium composition fire-lighting rod. Flints are also inexpensive, easy to use and light hundreds of times even after being fully submerged in water.

However, just carrying a good fire-lighting set with you is not enough. You must practise this until you can use it successfully in total darkness.

As a true survivor it is not good enough to just be able to create a flame – schoolchildren can do that. We need a fire.

Now practise getting a good fire going. Practise until proficient in that, too.

In your emergency survival kit always have at least one back-up fire-lighting method. I have a magnifying lens as a second and Condy's crystals and a glucose tablet as the third method in case it is overcast or night-time (which kills the magnifying lens method).

## Transporting fire

This may be necessary in certain circumstances, such as moving to a better location; or moving your camp fire due to rain, flooding or insect invasion. You will not be transporting fire, you will be transporting a fire *ember*.

It is virtually impossible to transport flames over a long distance, so don't risk trying it. Flames will go out or you could start a bushfire, creating a dangerous situation for yourself.

Cigarettes/cigars puffed gently is one way. Another proven method is placing the glowing red embers of hard charcoal bits in a tin can, with air holes to supply oxygen, and swinging it regularly to keep the coals glowing.

There are some bracket fungi that are superb at holding an ember and smouldering for many hours – experiment with any that may be growing in your area.

You can also make your own fire transport bundle in the shape and design of a large cigar. Roll your fine tinder in newspaper or paperbark and tie securely with string or vines. Light one end until it continuously smoulders. To stay burning it will require you to force oxygen into the centre of the bundle and this can be achieved by a swinging arm movement.

If travelling a long distance, make sure you take your original fire-making bits and pieces with you in case the transport embers go out. Remember, all methods will require a bundle of tinder to reignite your coals to flame again.

## CAMP FIRES

Nothing beats sitting around a camp fire – a good camp fire.

How do we create a good fire, whatever the reason?

Location: Out of the wind if possible.

On soft earth dig a hole in a shallow bowl shape, about 30 centimetres deep at the deepest point.

Place the dug-out sand on the windward side as a windbreak. There's no need to make a ring of stones. (Indeed, it's is best to not collect rocks, as these are the sheltered homes of geckos, spiders and micro-organisms, many of which will die or become predator food if exposed.)

Collect dry, dead branches from dead trees, or the above-ground limbs from fallen timber. (This again means that you are not destroying the valuable 'homes' of our little friends.) Choosing above-ground limbs means the wood will be drier and there will be less chance of infestation like termites. Solid timber burns hotter and for longer than rotten wood.

If the soil is damp create a 50-millimetre solid wooden buffer between the soil and your intended fire. Use thick, dry sticks.

I form up a teepee frame using strong sticks about a half-metre in length, driven into the soil to make the frame rigid. This allows me to lean lots of kindling sticks upright on it without the frame collapsing.

Bulk out the middle of the frame with your fine, dry tinder, then light the fire. The updraft is what we are after, and that teepee configuration is almost failsafe.

Once the fire is well established, lay on larger pieces of timber for your required level of comfort.

I always place two thick sticks leading out of the fire when I add more wood; these are escape routes for any lizards, insects and spiders etc. Kindness and respect.

> **WARNING:** Do not burn or cook on the dead wood from a poisonous plant because the toxins (in vapour form) can pollute your food, be absorbed into your water or cause you health concerns if inhaled.

When you have finished with your fire, pour water (usually used dishwashing water) over the coals, then bury with the excavated sand and contour smooth.

Sprinkle some leaf litter over the area, spread out the unused wood pile and depart, leaving the place as you found it.

## Camp fire etiquette

» Never throw anything into a cooking fire, especially if it is an Indigenous person's fire.
» The person who lights the fire owns the fire!
» It is really off-putting and offensive to throw cigarette butts or used tissues into a fire that someone may wish to use to cook a damper on. (Yes, it is sterile, but would you throw a used tissue in your kitchen oven while roasting the family's Sunday chicken meal? It's the same thing.)
» Do not add extra wood without the 'owner's' permission, as they may have wanted a low fire for some reason – again, respect.

# Chapter 11
# SHELTER

In hot or cold weather, your first line of defence is what you are wearing and what you are carrying. The quickest shelter to construct is usually the one you are carrying – a rescue blanket, poncho/raincoat or tent.

## RESCUE BLANKETS

There are many varieties available now through leading outdoor supply stores. They all work to a degree, with some better than others. Let the price be your guide to the quality of the item.

Emergency shelters, as we have said before, are essential for wellbeing and having a shelter with you in the form of a rescue blanket from the outset of any adventure is a tremendous bonus. As a waterproof, windproof garment, a rescue blanket could mean the difference between being comfortable or miserable or, in severe cases, between life or death.

The reverse side of a good emergency blanket should be an 'easy-to-see' red or orange colour that screams 'EMERGENCY!' and is in colour opposition to your surroundings, giving you the bonus of being a distress signal for ground or air searchers. The rescue blanket that you choose should be large enough for you to shelter under during the day, giving you 100 per cent shade (with the silver side up to reflect the heat) while acting as a magnificent giant sunlight reflector signal for searchers.

In cold weather you can simply wrap yourself in the blanket with the reflective side inward (which will reflect back approximately 80 per cent of your body heat). The good ones are also windproof and waterproof, therefore reducing the wind-chill factor.

Rescue blankets can also be used as a fire warmth-reflector, shaped in a configuration to reflect back heat from a fire, making you feel like a warm piece of toast.

## SHELTER CONSTRUCTION

I strongly suggest a 'teepee' dome shelter for cold or wet weather and a 'lean-to' with good air flow for hot or humid conditions. Both shapes are easy to construct and have been proven effective by indigenous peoples around the globe for millennia.

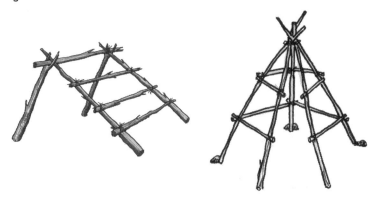

Plan out your construction first. Draw a sketch of the frame and then gather the correct amount and lengths of branches to suit – this saves energy and time. Start filling in the sides from the bottom up. This creates a natural water run-off for rain or heavy dew. You are only governed by the materials available and your imagination. The best materials to construct your walls or roof out of are sheets of bark and/or broad-leafed plants. These create the best wind/water proofing or shade for your effort.

Some common hazards to look out for when making shelters:

> » Check the trees you are considering building under for dead boughs. Known as 'widow makers', they will fall unpredictably and have caused serious injuries and death in the past.
> » Avoid all insect pathways and nests.
> » Never camp or shelter in the centre of a dry river bed, even if it isn't raining, because a flood upriver could catch you unawares.
> » The same applies to rain run-off areas: don't camp there.
> » In cold weather, build the door to your shelter on the protected side to help keep warmer and drier.
> » Do not shelter on or close to animal pathways.
> » Do not use poisonous plants in your shelter materials.

If you have your recommended three 10-centimetre-wide snake bite bandages or any similar, you can use these as extra cord for your knots or bindings in your shelter construction. Cut the bandages into 1-centimetre-wide strips and use these lengths. One bandage will give you 12.5 metres of good useable cordage.

## Shelter and signal combo

In order to be more visible to searchers, particularly from the air, you can make your shelter double as a signal – two for the energy price of one.

COMBINATION SHELTER AND SIGNAL:
'1 x effort = 2 x yield'

## Natural shelters

While caves and hollow tree trunks can keep you dry, and cool or warm, never forget that they can also hide or camouflage you from rescuers. If you do choose a natural shelter, make sure you leave notes and plenty of obvious attention-seeking signs that point to your whereabouts. A tripod of sticks with a note, including direction arrow and number of steps to your shelter, is a lifesaving idea.

Make very sure your new home is not the existing home of some other creatures which could harm or frighten you. It is essential to smoke out your new home as a deterrent to any unwanted visitors. The main concerns include snakes, wild dogs, wasps, bees, centipedes, scorpions, spiders, ants and bats.

## Cooking and food consumption areas

Never cook and/or eat where you are going to sleep. It attracts insects that attract small mammals that attract snakes. Wild dogs, dingoes and, in other countries, big cats and bears are all drawn to the odours of gutting and cooking of game. Prepare, cook and eat both away and downwind of your sleeping area. Predators are unwanted visitors, particularly when you are asleep and vulnerable.

## Shelter or protection using plastic bags

Split plastic bags and sew them together to make a waterproof and windproof shelter or create a heat reflector. Plastic bags can also be worn in three ways to help you stay dry, reduce wind-chill and help prevent heat loss from your body.

### Vest

Cut neck and arm holes and wear against drizzle or to combat a cool breeze.

### Hood

Just cut a hole for your face to provide extra protection from heavy rain and strong winds. This also retains maximum heat around your body.

## Poncho

This is useful for larger and/or taller people. It can be made by cutting along the seams, thus turning the bags into sheets. Join them by sewing or using canvas tape.

 OWL WISDOM: 'Do not overexert yourself. A crudely constructed shelter covering a healthy person is better than a perfectly built masterpiece covering an exhausted person' – my good friend Dave Alloway.

# Chapter 12
# DISTRESS SIGNALS

An amazing 90 per cent of people lost in Australia don't signal for help in any way, shape or form. They just carry on or move off without giving thought to how rescuers might locate them. It is distressing to realise that often a lot of wasted time, stress and, in some cases, loss of life could have been prevented by the simple acts of putting the vehicle bonnet up to indicate a mechanical problem; placing a note on the dashboard or on a stick tripod and arranging travel arrows on the ground before leaving the scene; or creating smoke signals.

**Two minutes** is the average time you have to successfully attract attention to yourself from when you first hear an approaching aircraft. Your life could depend on it, so make very

A Use

SOS
SMOKE
MIRROR
BONNET UP

Signals

sure you are ready to signal with whatever methods are available to you.

# NIGHT-TIME SIGNALS

## Signal flares

Three fires configured in an equilateral triangle are an internationally recognised night emergency signal. I prefer to call these 'signal flares' because if done correctly the volatile eruption of flames flare upwards for several metres, making it obvious that this is definitely not a camp fire – and easily seen kilometres away. To be effective these triangular emergency signal flares should be spaced at least 10 metres and not more than 30 metres apart.

A single-fire tripod flare is also a very effective night distress signal and is sometimes your only option in a confined space or with limited flammable materials.

To make a single signal flare, build a tripod of thick sticks, then create a platform halfway up and stuff the upper half with lots of dead leaves and dry grasses.

When you light this from beneath the platform, the updraught will cause the fire to flare into a large ball of flame visible from quite a distance.

## Flashing lights

Visual alerts at night can be also made with a series of three evenly spaced torch or camera flashes, followed by a pause and then repeated. A strobe light signal flashing continuously is designed to be a distress signal.

## Use your mobile

If a police chopper is looking for you, hold up your mobile phone, illuminate the face and point it towards the aircraft. Their night-vision goggles or screen will see it easily. If your phone has some battery power, try dialling 000 because this emergency number has a larger range than normal. Mobile phones with a GPS should be turned on even if out of communication range as they can be tracked by a satellite and your position located.

## Enhancing your night signals

One simple way to increase the chances of having your night signal seen is to amplify the light source by improvising a backing reflective screen. This can be achieved by having a reflective surface behind your light. Backing reflectors can be a mirror, CD or DVD discs, a sheet of aluminium foil, the inside of a beverage can, a wine cask bladder or the inside of a crisps packet; anything reflective. The silver side of a rescue blanket is a terrific aid when held behind your signal fire, torch or camera flashes. Even a Cyalume stick's glow will be magnified and much more easily seen.

## Tinsel tripod

Choose a prominent location and build a tripod as tall as is practicable. Decorate it with any object that is not normally found in nature. Preferably use things that reflect light and/or are colourful, such as empty bottles and cans, cutlery, CDs, rescue blankets and aluminium foil. Your tripod will attract attention because it is unusual.

If you have flagging tape, make firm, straight lines and add long hanging strips that will move in the breeze.

Remember to leave a note if you are not close by and arrows on the ground heading to your location.

If you do build it on a track or road, construct it so that it blocks the width. This will definitely make someone stop. At night, enhance your tripod with the number plates from your car and hang any garments with reflective strips on them. Headlights and searchlights will certainly spot these.

## DAYTIME SIGNALS

You can use the same reflective surfaces to signal with the sun's light as you can at night – any CD or DVD, a sheet of aluminium foil, the inside of a beverage can, a shiny wine cask bladder or even a credit card.

You can also use the mirror from your kit or any other mirror – your car has three. Mirror flashes in particular are blinding. They have been seen over 20 kilometres.

### Using a mirror to signal
**Method 1**
This is known as the 'rifle sight' technique. Shine reflected sunlight towards the back of your extended hand, through the 'V' of your first two

fingers. Remove your hand and the flash should be exactly on the target.

## Method 2
Shine the reflection on the ground and move it in a straight line from the ground to your target and then flash the mirror at the target.

When using either method, aim just in front of the plane or vehicle so it moves into your flashes. This gives you the best chance of being seen. Waggling the mirror slightly will also increase the chances.

## Opportunistic signalling
Using your mirror from a high vantage point, simply pan through the full 360-degree radius of the horizon. Doing this increases your chances of attracting attention to yourself. These random flashes may be seen by ground search parties or by other people in the area. When resting or doing chores, keep the signalling going by hanging your mirror off a tall, leaning stick on a string, allowing it to spin.

## Smoke signals
Smoke signals are still as effective today as they were 1000 years ago.

They can be seen many kilometres away, particularly by aircraft. Ground searchers can also smell the smoke from long distances. Good smoky fires from natural resources can be achieved by setting up your signal flare fire tripod as you would for a night signal. After stuffing the top half with combustible materials, cover that section with green tree branches. To create more smoke once you have lit the fire, let it start to burn, then throw on pre-cut branches of green leaves, smothering the flames. This creates copious amounts of smoke. The updraft of flames will help raise the smoke above tree height.

Be clever and cut the green branches with a 'hook' on the end to attach them onto the fire.

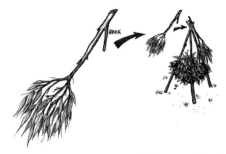

If you have access to a vehicle, totally deflate the spare tyre and burn that first because tyres give off copious thick, black smoke for a long time. Deflating the tyre means its air will not expand and explode in the intense heat and it will therefore pose no danger to bystanders. The easiest way to deflate it is to remove the tube's valve by twisting it out in an anticlockwise direction or stab the tyre wall in several places.

The strong smell of burning rubber can also be detected by searchers, which could lead them to you.

A cameraman, filming sunsets for a local TV station in Perth, saved his own life by using his tyres as fuel for a distress signal in a very remote and hot part of the Gascoyne region of Western Australia. He attended one of my courses and remembered this method after a short panic attack when he realised that his brand-new 4WD was not going to start – its computer system had died. He wasn't due back in Perth for a week and had limited water. On day 2 the people working on a nearby sheep station saw the smoke for a second time. They realised it could be a distress signal and went to investigate – he believes that saved his life.

## GROUND-TO-AIR SOS MESSAGES

Still the most effective in the world is the word 'HELP'. It's easy to read and very easy to mark out with square letters.

Write the letters in a big open area. Create as much contrast as possible between the letters and the surrounding ground colour as you can. Materials used for contrast can be branches, shrubs, rocks, seaweed, engine or diff oils, newspaper sheets or toilet paper pegged down, clothing and tarps.

Make big, square-sided letters – they have been proven to attract attention more easily than round or curved letters.

You can even shovel a trench with all the sand piled on one side of each letter to enhance its visibility by creating a shadow.

Use smoke and/or mirror flashes to bring the pilot's attention to your message.

## AUDIBLE SOUND SIGNALS

Three whistle blasts, evenly spaced, can be heard over a long distance and even further at night. It is a much more effective, more energy saving and less distressing method than shouting for help.

Anything else that creates a reasonably loud sound can be used to alert people's attention to you.

Car-horn beeps, hubcaps or two metal pots banged together, rifle shots, hollow trees or logs used like a drum, two empty glass bottles clanged together – make all these noises in sets of three.

> **NOTE:** Searchers should give one long whistle blast periodically when looking for someone lost. Two reasons for this: firstly the missing person may be lying down and resting or sleeping. Secondly they may be just in front of the rescuers, walking at the same speed.

## WRITTEN MESSAGES AND NOTES

» If you decide to move away from your chosen base camp area or vehicle to search for water, food, shelter or signal construction material, always leave a clearly printed note placed in a very obvious and prominent position. If you are in wet conditions, seal the message in a plastic bag.

# TEMPLATE FOR EMERGENCY NOTE

## HELP
### PLEASE HELP – THIS IS AN EMERGENCY

Today's date: ................................. Time: .................. AM or PM

My full name is: ....................................................................

Age: ...........

The names and ages of people with me are:

................................................................................

................................................................................

................................................................................

................................................................................

................................................................................

The reason I/we are stranded: ................................................

................................................................................

................................................................................

................................................................................

The reason for leaving is: ......................................................

................................................................................

................................................................................

................................................................................

The direction I/we have left in is: ..........................................

This direction is marked with an arrow drawn on the ground.

My/our intended plan is to walk to: .................................................

.................................................................................................

.................................................................................................

I/we have a total of ............... litres of water with us.

The list of gear or supplies we will be carrying when we leave is:

.................................................................................................

.................................................................................................

.................................................................................................

My/our clothing colours are: ....................................................

My/our physical and medical condition is: ......................................

.................................................................................................

.................................................................................................

.................................................................................................

You can best help me/us by: ....................................................

.................................................................................................

.................................................................................................

Extra information that may help you help me is: ...........................

.................................................................................................

.................................................................................................

.................................................................................................

Below or on the back of this note is a sketch map of my intentions.

» In a vehicle, leave your message on the steering wheel or windscreen – with your car bonnet up. Leave a distress message at any windmill you visit, because it will be periodically maintained and could lead to an earlier rescue.

» Remember to always leave large arrows marked on the ground indicating the direction you have taken.

» More notes can be made by using charcoal for writing on any light-coloured surface, such as flat rocks or white bark from trees.

» Use toilet paper to enhance and attract attention to your note.

» You can write comprehensive messages on flagging tape with a pen or felt pen.

» Leave several messages if possible.

OWL WISDOM: When people are searching for you, signals could be the lifesaving difference. Never give up hope and never stop trying.

# EMERGENCY BEACONS AND SATELLITE PHONES

Emergency position indicating radio beacons (EPIRB) are used in emergency situations to assist Search and Rescue organisations locate people who are in a potentially life-threatening situation on land, sea or air.

These tracking transmitters, also known as distress beacons or emergency beacons, now transmit on the dedicated 406 MHz frequency.

There are two other types of distress beacons: the emergency locator transmitters (ELT), which are fitted in all aircraft, and the personal locator beacon (PLB) for personal use in an emergency.

All three are highly effective and I recommend every group or solo person should have an EPIRB or PLB when travelling or working in remote areas or on the ocean.

When activated they pulse out a distress signal that, when detected by satellites, can triangulate the sender's location almost instantly within 100 square metres, and all your registered information is immediately available for all Search and Rescue land, sea or air search parties.

You are required to register your details (including trip itinerary) when you purchase or hire an EPIRB. This service is free and can be changed or updated online. EPIRBs are moderate in price or can be hired.

All these distress signals are only to be used if you believe your life or some else's life is in danger.

There are thousands of accidental signals sent each year by poorly managed beacons placed in vulnerable positions that activate them unnecessarily – or by children playing with them.

Store beacons in a watertight container and treat with

respect, as non-essential searches are very costly and waste the time of Search and Rescue.

Satellite phones can be bought or hired for remote journeys and now are reliable in open areas (not guaranteed in gorges or in extremely overcast periods of weather). Using a sat phone allows you to give more information in an emergency. You have the ability to call the Royal Flying Doctor Service (RFDS), hospital or your doctor for medical advice. You can also call and reassure someone if you are only running late for your expected return or rendezvous.

Even with an EPIRB and/or satellite phone you must consider the amount of time it will take rescuers or someone to find and assist you. There are massive remote areas that are too far for a helicopter to fly out to and return from, due to their fuel capacity. Also, many areas lack airstrips for light aircraft to land.

Numerous airstrips marked on maps are subserviced and not usable by any aircraft, particularly the faster and larger RFDS planes.

Think of how long it took (or would take) for you to drive out to your chosen remote destination. Six days? Then it would take a SAR (Search and Rescue) team that long as well. Have you taken enough food, water and extra special medications to last that long or longer?

Back to 'Plan B' strategies: plan carefully for trips whether on foot or any form of vehicle.

 OWL WISDOM: Learn and lean on your basic survival knowledge. Your battery-driven devices should only be a backup to your survival skills.

# Chapter 13
# FOOD FOR THOUGHT

The longest I have gone without food is four and a half days, and from that and other experiences and observations I can assure you that you wouldn't feel hungry in a real survival situation. Anxiety will override hunger every time.

Trust me, you will not feel hungry when you are lost or stranded. Even on my controlled advanced courses I have to remind people to eat something after the first 24 hours. Their fears of 'what might happen' overrule hunger. It is almost unbelievable to think someone can miss out on three or more meals and still not have the desire to eat. However, I believe you should have some form of food in your emergency kit.

If you were stranded with me in the wilderness today, from my survival kit I could offer you chicken or beef soup tonight, followed by sweet tea or coffee. That sounds more like being in control to me than eating a handful of grubs. All my survival kit menu choices will smell and taste like something familiar and comforting to you. This creates the feeling that you have at least some form of control over what's happening to you in this strange and unfamiliar scene. This could be the key to keeping your thoughts positive and optimistic. To my way of thinking, this is the real reason for eating in such situations. It is not food for hunger – it is food for thought.

Let's look at the three ways to obtain food in the wild: fishing, hunting and foraging.

Of the three, fishing is the best way to find a reasonably nourishing meal with little skill and without expending a lot of precious energy.

## FISHING HINTS

» Fish in the deepest section of the river or the waterhole.
» Cast your line into the shaded or shadowed areas which the larger fish use for concealment. Don't let your lone body silhouette be the only shape on the water's edge; this can scare off fish.
» Cut a pole to gain easy line entry over snags, such as tree roots and rocky areas. Make an improvised gaff on a stick using a spare hook – just in case you catch an unexpected whopper, which is a real possibility in remote locations.

To kill a fish, use a round, hard stick and hit hard on an imaginary equilateral triangle apex point above the eyes, using the eye width as a base line. This is the most humane way to dispatch a fish.

Survivalists en route to a potential fishing spot would be gathering bait as they walked in the form of grasshoppers, grubs or dried meat from a dead animal carcass, as well as feathers or hair tufts to make lures. Red seems to be the favoured colour as a lure for our inland fish, especially perch.

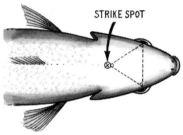

STRIKE SPOT

If you intertwine sticky spider web between a forked stick this can then be used to catch flying insects for bait, in the same way you would use a scoop net.

I have always been able to catch fish with some of the contents from my survival kit used as lures.

**OWL WISDOM:** There hasn't been a death from starvation in a survival situation in Australia in the last 100 years or more. It's always been from dehydration and/or exposure. Make sure the priorities of water, warmth, shelter and signals are well satisfied before hunger.

# HUNTING

I am not against people who hunt respectfully and lawfully for some tucker; in fact, I think it's a good thing. There is a great deal to learn and we also get to realise that something really does have to die for us to consume it with gravy and vegies. There is no pleasure in taking something's life force and no pleasure in gutting something – there is only physical work in preparing the carcass for the pot – no glory.

From my experiences of being the 'hunter' I know hunting is an art that takes years to perfect and even longer to achieve guaranteed results. An untrained hunter will either get hungry quicker or get hurt; therefore, we should be happy and content in a survival situation to be gatherers.

Before considering spending time and, more importantly, energy on a hunting expedition in your survival situation, explore local vegetarian options first. From my experience there are always some plant foods available, in all areas, in all seasons.

If you do kill an animal for food, make sure you gut and skin it and then *overcook* it. The emphasis on overcooking your food is to ensure that any heat-tolerant bacteria or cysts or other parasites are killed before consumption.

If you make soup from animals you have caught and killed, make sure to boil it very well before consuming it, for the same reasons as above.

You can cook fish with their guts still intact in the hot coals of a fire, but if you have pierced the stomach or intestines with a spear, arrow, gaff or knife then you need to gut them and thoroughly wash out the remaining cavity.

If not, the flesh could taste terrible or be contaminated with nasty bacteria.

# FORAGING

Trees and shrubs don't move as fast, so you will have no difficulty at all in catching them as a food source. You can live very satisfactorily on vegetation alone and that has been proven many times over by survivors.

## Handle with care

However, when it comes to bush tucker from plants, we must be very careful to ensure that what we sample is the right plant and not a poisonous lookalike – that is obvious, but plant poisoning still occurs on a daily basis.

What is often not so obvious is that we can poison ourselves in a number of other accidental ways:

» Handling some toxic plants with your bare hands can expose your skin to the pure resin, which can be absorbed into your body.

» Kebab sticks made out of poisonous plant stems can poison your food from resin absorption.

» If you handle caustic plants you may transfer that resin to your eyes and cause mild to severe problems.

» Red seeds made into bush jewellery have transferred enough toxin to make the wearer ill.

» Even smelling the flowers of highly toxic plants can cause terrible headaches.

- » Rashes and allergic reactions from some stinging plants can occur on any part of your exposed body, when brushed against them. (Another reason to wear long trousers and long-sleeved shirts in the bush.)
- » Do not place plastic bags over toxic plant branches to get fresh drinking water using the transpiration method – you will poison the water.
- » Boiling water too is susceptible to becoming tainted by absorbing resins in vapour foam, often making the water unpalatable as well as poisonous.
- » Fumes from burning poisonous plants, if inhaled, are so toxic that they can be lethal in a confined space. The fumes from burning oleander (a highly toxic introduced shrub that has invaded bushland in some areas) in their lounge room open fire nearly killed a family of four in NSW. They were saved by an unexpected visiting family friend.

**EXTREMELY IMPORTANT: Do not burn or cook on the dead wood from any poisonous plant. The toxins emitted in vapour form can be absorbed into your food while it is cooking.**

## My Universal Taste Test

To minimise the risk of accidental poisoning I have developed seven steps that I call my 'Universal Taste Test'. I have personally found the poison indicators very useful in avoiding potential hazards from contact with toxic plants in the USA, UK, Africa and the jungles of

Indonesia. All suspicious plants later proved to be indeed toxic (100 per cent correct from just the physical indicators). This test is designed as part of a long-term survival strategy, to prevent accidental poisoning from utilising plants in a variety of ways, not just as an edibility test. When followed correctly it should prevent any mishaps with toxic plant parts worldwide; however, there are no guarantees.

You must carry out every step on the part of the plant that you intend to use.

## 1. The 'look' test

Actively look for poison indicators. There are exceptions, but the following physical indicators are a reliable guide to whether a plant is poisonous:

- » Red seeds
- » Opposite leaf or leaflet shapes
- » Palmate leaves
- » Milky sap
- » Prickly fruits
- » Furry stems
- » Trumpet- or bell-shaped flowers
- » Pea flowers
- » Avoid all fungi

## 2. The 'smell' test

Crush the portion of the plant that you are considering eating or using and sniff it to detect aromatic odours:

- » Almond or peach-like odours may be an indicator of natural cyanide
- » Unpleasant odours usually indicate that the plant is not edible

### 3. The 'skin' test

» If it passes the 'look' and 'smell' tests, then crush a small portion of the plant (the part you are thinking of eating/using) and rub onto your wrist just above where a watchband sits. Your wrist is a sensitive part of your body that you can afford to sacrifice to experimentation.

» Wait 15 minutes. If there is any kind of reaction, such as itching, swelling, redness or pain on the skin, discard the plant – do not eat it.

### 4. The 'lip' test

Rub a little of the crushed plant that passed the test on your wrist on to the inside of the very corner of your bottom lip. Do not rub it in the middle of your lip, as it may have a burning or irritating effect, making further eating and drinking difficult. Wait 15 minutes. If there are any adverse reactions *whatsoever*, discard the plant - do not eat it.

### 5. The 'tongue' test

If there is still no adverse reaction, roll a small portion into a little ball shape and rotate it on and under your tongue – then spit it out. This allows all the sensory sections of your tongue a chance to discover any adverse reaction or sensation. Wait another 15 minutes and confirm there is no form of irritation or awful taste received from any part of your tongue or mouth. Again, if *any* unpleasant sensations occur, do not continue.

### 6. The 'swallow' test

At this stage you can swallow a portion no bigger than the size of a small grape. This time you must wait four hours to check for bad reactions, such as headache, nausea, diarrhoea, fever or cramps, in any part of your body. Do not consume any other food during these four hours. Again, if there are any unpleasant sensations or reactions, do not continue.

## 7. The final step – the 'eat' test

If you experienced no ill-effects while performing any of these tests, then you can slowly increase the amounts you consume – proceed by doubling the amount consumed and again waiting four hours, then increase portions in small amounts.

## Universal plant poison indicators

| | | |
|---|---|---|
| Furry Stems | Opposite Leaves | Fungi |
| Milky Sap | Palmate Leaves | Red Seeds |
| Trumpet/Bell Flowers | Pea Flowers | Prickly Fruit |

## Why not fungi?

Some toxins in fungi can take more than 12 hours to react in your metabolism and therefore *cannot* be detected in my Universal Taste Test. In some cases these reactions on humans have been harmful, and even dangerous.

Yes, we have native truffles and magnificent mushrooms growing wild in Australia but please be cautious with all fungi, because every fungus that is edible (including mushrooms) has a deadly version that is almost identical. I cannot stress enough to you that incorrectly identified fungi when consumed have caused severe to fatal reactions in people. Amanita species grow in Australia and are often found growing amongst field mushrooms.

Before I came up with any form of taste test, I ate a very small piece of bracket fungi that smelt okay and was growing in the Dwellingup forest in Western Australia. Within one hour I had the dual symptoms of violent projectile vomiting and diarrhoea – exceedingly unpleasant. If I had been in a real survival situation and had to rely on my focus and mobility I would have been in serious trouble.

IMPORTANT: Different people have allergic reactions to different plant properties, so the Universal Taste Test must always be carried out by every person wishing to eat any part of an unfamiliar plant. The process must never be cut short.

REMEMBER: There are exceptions to all these rules – if in doubt, leave alone!

# Chapter 14
# PLANNING FOR SURVIVAL

Many more people and groups are now venturing into our wilderness, and why not? We live in one of the most spectacularly beautiful places on earth.

Consider the following scenario. You are the leader of a group of five teenagers, one of whom has just sustained a knee injury, is in constant pain and can now only move very slowly. And you realise you are lost.

Your satellite phone doesn't have reception due to excessive cloud cover and your GPS battery is flat. With an intense storm due tomorrow, you now have to make some decisions – what the hell are they?

First thoughts are usually based on fear, and usually the fear of loss:

» Loss of credibility – ego – what will people think of me now?
» Fear of being lost itself
» The loss of life – worst-case scenario

There are plenty more fears. Sadly, though, most of these emotional fears cannot help you make any good, clear, positive decisions, unless by accident. In an emergency situation I ask you to be extremely rational. Of course you will be emotional but please do not let this override rational solutions based on the knowledge you have.

# MAKE A 'PLAN B'

When placed in such unanticipated circumstances, I believe you should halt proceedings immediately and take control both physically and rationally.

First, make the entire group comfortable by sheltering from the weather, even if conditions are mild. This means they can rest while you think.

Next step is to create an atmosphere in which you can actually think and plan properly. Someone's life could depend on the decisions you make for their immediate future.

Organise a central camp fire and have a brew of coffee or tea. This action will calm your nerves, to a degree, and puts other people's minds and hands to work, and off worry.

In this scenario you are lost and have an injured person who is uncomfortable, due to being in pain. How can you tackle those problems with possible options and solutions?

While in a somewhat more relaxed state, write down your ideas. Do not just rely on memory, because your mind is already in overload; also, writing on paper helps you focus.

If it appears that you will exhaust your supplies or resources then plan for basic survival.

If that is the case, write down the five principal priorities for survival (Water, Warmth, Shelter, Signals and Food). Place them in order of importance in your situation, and include the injury and the fact that you are lost. Now write down the ways you can respond to each of those needs and concerns and prioritise them again. This should start to clarify how to spend your energy, resources and time wisely.

Plenty to think about and plenty to plan – and you haven't finished your coffee yet. By simply taking some action and some control of the physical situation our minds tend to follow a more logical and calmer path. At least you have done something positive and set a scene that dampens fear in all with you, and most of all for the decision maker – you.

Keep thinking and keep planning until you have your Plan B – always be flexible. (Plan A was what you were on before you got lost.) You are allowed to have a Plan C and more. In most survival situations you have at least time in your favour. (Remember that in this scenario there is a storm scheduled for tomorrow.)

## Goal setting

This is extremely important – you must have goals to aim for. Short, achievable goals can turn a seemingly insurmountable task into an attainable one. Celebrate each goal achieved as you move closer to your ultimate goal. Celebrating with just a round of applause, song or a 'Yahoo!' will lift morale amazingly. I do this celebrating 'trick' on every long journey I undergo, even road trips and interstate flights. Each step or phase closer to my destination I celebrate, often with a snack or coffee or, if in no other way, then mentally to myself.

Now bring the group together and deliver your thoughts for Plan B and ask all members to think of any more ideas. Be careful not to burden your mind with nonsense opinions – you need common sense, not guesswork.

Once you have considered their input and formed your plan, announce your new strategy of action, then prioritise the tasks and delegate the labour.

In your scenario you decide to camp overnight and rest the injured person. He was given painkillers and anti-inflammatory medication. Everyone has a good night's sleep. One of the group's members had batteries that fitted your GPS and in the morning you were able to position yourself accurately on your map. As a group you walked out 500 metres to your chosen emergency exit track with the injured person using an improvised crutch. You were then able to engage sat phone reception from an open space on the track. You phoned your backup person who picked you all up in her 4WD troop carrier just before the storm. Plan B worked!

Too many people don't plan their outings or their way out of mistakes and mishaps. They just rely on luck. My definition of luck is when good planning meets an opportunity.

## An ABC for survival

A accept the situation as it is
B brew a beverage and drink it
C consider all factors and priorities
D decide a plan of action
E execute your plan – however, be flexible

# THE IMPORTANCE OF PLANNING AHEAD

Do the words 'If only …' sound familiar?

The amount of money, volunteer time and nervous energy spent looking for the lost by searchers is enormous and the extreme worry suffered by loved ones is staggering.

The volunteers from Search and Rescue, the police and other government agencies are all out there, usually in awful weather conditions and in isolated areas, looking for someone who was ill-prepared – only occasionally is injury or illness the cause for rescue. Accountable risk management is what we are talking about. Sometimes people venture out with a lack of knowledge or are just ill-informed, but if someone who knows better ventures into a remote area anywhere in the world without a contingency plan, has a mishap, then relies totally on someone else helping them, I would tag that attitude as disrespectful and irresponsible. If it is an adult, then add 'foolish'.

# PLAN FOR WORST-CASE SCENARIOS

Prior to the event, study your journey's route and think of 'what ifs' and worst-case scenarios and have a plan in place for those. I suggest breaking the trip up into half-day sections and on your map note the emergency exit direction, distance and mark flat areas where a chopper could land (with LZ for landing zone) to evacuate a sick or injured person. Make a note of the helicopter company's phone numbers, plus other local emergency services phone numbers, the nearest hospital, etc. Refer to the list of main emergency numbers on page 230. Write these important numbers on the back of your main map or in your notebook. Do all of this in the comfort of your home (perhaps in your own study room), with no pressure and no distractions.

## HAVE AN ESCAPE ROUTE

As the organiser, have a cardinal compass direction as an emergency exit plan. This would be to a main track, or some other linear feature on the map which is accessible by vehicle. Individuals or groups in trouble or lost can be instructed to navigate out to that track and wait for help. Look for these escape routes when planning your expedition. If the area doesn't have one, then think 'Is it worth it?' and perhaps choose another area.

If you plan beforehand, you will already have a Plan B ready if a problem arises. Of course, there may be unforeseen incidents from time to time, but your existing emergency plans will simplify your decisions if you need to make a new plan.

When I'm the organiser I also deliver those plans for all participants to copy in the briefing prior to departure.

I also get everyone to make their own sketch of the entire course, with distances and main features marked en route. There are good reasons behind the effort. One is that it stops people asking the person with the real maps lots of questions that they can now answer themselves. If the original maps get lost you all have a copy. If one participant gets separated from the group they have a form of map on them and, lastly, all participants have peace of mind in knowing what's going on.

# DESERT DEATH – A MESSAGE

In my acknowledgements I mention Oyers Pander, who at the age of 31 was prospecting for gold. His vehicle became bogged on a sand track and he perished from dehydration in 44°C heat in the Great Sandy Desert. He had left behind all his emergency gear at his tent and base camp, more than 20 kilometres away. He was bogged with a possible maximum of 4 litres of drinking water in this isolated desert area, in extreme heat; this is not a good scenario. Being in an unfamiliar area adds more mental stress. Oyers made the decision to leave his vehicle and headed west along the same track to where a waterhole is marked on all maps of that area.

A grader driver, working on the main dirt road that Oyers had turned off, spotted the bogged vehicle 500 metres away and thought someone might be camping there. The next day he observed the vehicle in the same spot and drove over to inspect. There was no note or any other sign to tell him someone was in need of help, the bonnet was down and the car was locked. However he felt uneasy and reported his findings to the nearest police station that night. Due to the distance from a town, another two days lapsed before the police did an aerial plane search. Then a ground search on day 3 discovered Oyers' body 5.7 kilometres from his bogged vehicle. That was as far as the local police thought he had walked before dying.

While the aerial search was still underway, I was asked by the ABC regional radio station if the missing person could still be alive. My answer was: 'Depends if he has adequate water; lack of food is not an issue'. After the discovery of his body I felt uneasy as I studied the circumstances and believed something was wrong because of the short distance it was assumed he walked before perishing. I had a desire to investigate and that opportunity manifested itself a few weeks later.

I was conducting a survival course at Telfer, a mine site near the scene of this tragedy. I was driven out there by the mine safety officer and I was able to track Oyers' movements. I found his makeshift overnight camp, his footwear, hat, and some empty food tins. Recent newspaper reports had stated in error, 'He must have been inexperienced and foolish to be out there without a hat and footwear'. I discovered another clue and deduced that Oyers died returning from the waterhole marked on his map, not on the way to it as had been reported. What I noticed was a piece of light-blue polystyrene foam stuck in the end of a dead branch hanging partially on the track and I believe Oyers did that. He could only have left that trace of evidence on the way back to his vehicle by accidently brushing his water container against the tree branch. He had an idea to walk to that waterhole 8 kilometres away – not a bad choice, as no one would miss him for several weeks. He walked there but unfortunately did not interpret what he saw correctly. He failed to locate the waterhole.

I went down to the edge of the dry river bed and sat in an obvious spot anyone would have sat and rested. I then realised his mistake. He didn't find the waterhole because it was obscured behind a well established island of sand, shrubs and trees several hundred metres long and 300 metres out into the dry river system.

Very old wheel tracks could be seen crossing the dry river sand and up onto that island. That gave a false impression that this was the full width of the river. If you really studied the map you would notice the river was much wider and the blue dot was indeed hugging the west side bank. If only he had been a bit more coherent. Behind this sit spot was his discarded shirt and a small compass. When I held them in my hands I felt a deep, deep sorrow. To make my feelings worse I could hear the galahs squawking their heads off, giving the lifesaving waterhole's location away a few hundred metres west. Did he not hear them or was he here in the middle of the day when all is quiet? I walked over to the water-hole on the other side of the island. This day was also extremely hot and I was sweating. I looked into the crystal clear, waist-deep water teeming with small fish and just sat thinking 'How terrible'. I have never felt so sad at a waterhole before. All I could do was imagine the pain and anguish Oyers would have suffered – and think 'If only!'

Altogether that is the true story of his demise.

As I was being driven back to Telfer we were driving past the place where Oyers's body was found when I heard a loud voice say 'Thank you'. It startled me because it was it was incredibly loud and clear. No one else in the car heard that voice. I believe it was a message was from Oyers – for now someone knew he was not foolish. I instantly realised why he 'spoke 'to me. I had the evidence that he was not a fool – just a person trying to make decisions under great stress and who made some mistakes.

Now many years later I know, and his spirit knows, that his death has not been a complete waste because when I deliver the lessons in observation and preparedness on every survival course, I do so with Oyers in mind. We know that those lessons may save someone's life in a similar situation.

**OWL WISDOM:**
- **Deflate tyres to prevent bogging your car–, this gives a larger 'footprint' and the softer rubber has a better grip in sand or mud**
- **Best option is usually to stay with your vehicle**
- **Do not get separated from your emergency supplies**
- **Leave notes for rescuers**
- **Put up bonnet on vehicles as part of your distress signals**
- **Use seed-eating birds' flight patterns and calls to locate water**
- **Many insects are water-dependent and don't stray far from their water source**
- **Always carry extra water**

**OWL WISDOM: Think of your own safety and the mental anguish of others who care about you. Take precautions; too many people have perished already.**

# WOMEN IN THE WILD

As a person who conducts outback survival courses and has done so for three decades I am seeing more and more women attend my courses.

All you men rmember that real survival is not about how physically tough you are.

Knowledge is what we all need. Knowledge is empowering and this helps anyone, anywhere, in situations when we need to put emotions aside and make rational decisions in a timely manner.

There are many reasons for individuals and families to be in a potential survival situation, and having the know-how to 'nut out' a strategy for success may fall on the shoulders of the last person standing – and if that's the partner of a badly injured or ill person then she and she alone has this responsibility for her partner, and in some cases the whole family as well.

Women are equal to men in all survival subjects – and in many cases perform better because they are less competitive, more able to listen, and have a group survival mentality.

The peace of mind gained from such knowledge cannot be measured.

# Chapter 15
# SURVIVING ON THE COAST

## SHORELINE SHOPPING

Shorelines at low tide are a terrific place to fossick, and a particularly great shopping centre for food and utensils in a survival situation.

There are plenty of edible shellfish. The part we eat is the main muscle or foot, and many of these are flavoursome and nourishing.

Below are several alternative cooking methods for seafood in a survival situation.

All live shells and sea creatures within Australian waters are protected and this needs to be respected. If you wish to practise these methods then purchase your supply from a fish market.

> » Shells (molluscs): Place all the shells upside down in wet, firm sand and burn a very quick hot fire over the top. The fire should be as intense as possible and should only last for three minutes. Let the shells cool off and winkle

out the muscle section with a pointed stick. Remove the entrails (guts and intestines) and reproductive organs, rinse in salt water and consume. This method cooks the flesh in its own juices and retains a lot more flavour.

» Method 2 for shells: Simply cook the shells in boiling water as you would with chicken eggs. With bivalves – the most common of these being mussels and cockles – the rule is that if they do not open, they were already dead before cooking and are poisonous. You can eat the ones that do open, but do not use the boiled water as soup – one dead shell could turn your 'soup' toxic.

» Use radiated heat from a fire with the shells lined up on the edge of the fireplace. The heat will cook the shells. Turn them over with wooden tongs and when they 'open up' they are cooked. I particularly like fresh oysters prepared this way.

» You can cook crabs, octopuses and lobsters in boiling water – kill them first.

» You can also cook them in the hot coals of a fire the same way you would cook a fish. To start with, construct a large fire using hard woods to create a mound of hot coals big enough to bury and cook your fresh seafood. Scrape off all the coals, leaving just a bed of hot sand. Always kill the fish, crabs, octopuses or lobsters first before cooking, then place them on the bed of hot sand and completely cover with the hot coals. Finally, add a layer of sand on top, to keep in the heat. Depending upon the size of the food, bake for no more than 20 minutes. Remember, with all seafoods you can eat them raw, so do not overcook – same applies to home cooking.

## Useful shore finds

Fossicking at the high tide mark on any beach will reward you with a lot of useful gear in a survival situation. The list is endless but I have found jars half full of foods like jam and peanut paste – still consumable – whole fishing rigs, bottles and large, dead, cleaned-out conch and bailer shells (ideal for cooking or transporting water). I have seen pieces of bailer and conch shell 160 kilometres inland from the coast, remnants left by Aboriginal people using them as bowls and/or water-carrying containers.

Other useful items may include shiny or contrasting coloured items for signalling, and seaweed and rubber products which can be used to produce attention-seeking black smoke from a signal fire. You can often find enough materials to create a distilling plant, turning the abundant sea water supply into fresh water. I witnessed this as an instructor with one group of five Special Forces soldiers on their survival course in 2002. They produced enough drinking water for the group to stay healthy for three days. They used one of their steel mugs as the salt-water boiling container, with some form of aluminium foil as a cone-shaped lid and about a metre of coiled plastic hose in damp sand, condensing the steam into fresh drinking water. This water then dribbled into a foraged glass bottle at the rate of 1 litre per hour – excellent improvising and result.

If stranded on the coast, create or draw the large square letters of SOS or HELP on the shoreline. This will eventually be seen by Coast Watch or any other plane that may be hugging the coastline.

Coast Watch is a government surveillance organisation. Their planes do regular sweeps along even the remotest parts of the continent while looking for any illegal activities. Ground-to-air signals from stranded people have been seen and reported by Coast Watch. That has saved lives in the past and, I am sure, will save more in the future.

# HARMFUL COASTAL CREATURES

The Australian coastline and the shallow waters adjacent can present a number of hazards that could maim or even kill you – or at the very least, ruin your visit – if not recognised and avoided.

The following sections introduce the most significant of these, and cover their recognition, precautions to be taken, signs and symptoms of injury, and treatment.

## Stingrays (Myliobatoidei)

Stingrays resting lie motionless on the bottom, covered with sand, camouflaging themselves so that it is very difficult for you to see them. If you tread on one or swim over one in shallow water and it feels threatened, the stingray will lash upwards with its tail, thrusting the spine, or barb, into your leg or body. It may do so repeatedly, causing terrible wounds and in extreme cases death – as in the sad case of Steve Irwin. Stingrays are often caught on lines and sometimes in nets.

### *Recognition*

Stingrays have 1–2 venomous barbs on their tails. In the most dangerous species, these barbs are near the tail end, like a scorpion. The barb is double-edged and tapered, with a row of backward-pointing serrations on each side to tear flesh on withdrawal. This assists venom absorption. You can eat stingray wings and some species are considered a delicacy.

### Precautions
» If caught on a line, a stingray should be rolled over onto its back against a boat hull or on its back when on the beach to cut the line or remove the hook – it cannot bend its tail beneath itself.
» The same applies if caught in a net – roll the stingray onto its back and cut it out of the net.
» When wading in shallow water over sand or mud flats, shuffle your feet – this will disturb the ray and you will avoid stepping on it.
» Never swim directly over a resting stingray in shallow water.

### Signs and symptoms
» Usually a very large wound, with severe bleeding.
» Extreme pain that can lead to shock.

### Treatment
» Irrigate the wound site with copious amounts of water.
» Arrest the bleeding and be prepared to treat for possible shock.
» If the barb breaks off do not pull it out – that is a hospital task.
» Transport to a medical centre for treatment and medical cleaning of the wound.

## Stonefish (Synanceiidae)

The stonefish is found in the northern half of Australia's coastline. It is the deadliest of our venomous fishes, having been responsible for a considerable number of fatalities. Although commonly known as the estuarine stonefish, it is also found in exposed rock pools, far from estuaries.

It has a particularly efficient method of injecting venom. Slight pressure on any of the 13 dorsal spines causes the contents of the venom glands to be expelled through the hypodermic spine's tip. By this means a stonefish can inject the entire contents of venom into your foot or hand at just the slightest touch. The more spines involved, the more severe the pain.

### *Recognition*

The stonefish can grow up to 60 centimetres long, but the usual length is 20–30 centimetres. It's a sluggish fish that relies on camouflage to avoid detection and to swallow any unwary small fish swimming by. It can be caught on a fishing line, in a gill net or trawled up in a net. The most common cause of envenomation is an innocent fossicker treading on one.

### Precautions

» Never attempt to pick one up by hand.

» Often dead ones are found in the high-tide weed line. These are still potentially deadly.

» When walking in shallows, wear stout-soled footwear. Tread in sandy spots and shuffle your feet. You can see them if you keep a sharp eye on where you are placing your feet.

» Take care when sorting the catch of a net.

» Divers, be very cautious where you place your hands, especially on muddy or stone reefs.

» If you catch one on a line, with much caution cut the line off at least 30 centimetres above the fish. The hook will rust out.

### Signs and symptoms

» Immediate, excruciating pain, spreading along the limb.

» Shock can develop very quickly.

### Treatment

» Get the person out of the water.

» Get ready to treat for shock.

» Immerse the limb in hot/warm water. Heat applied can alleviate the pain to a tolerable level.

» Use any available hot liquid – even coffee, tea or soup – poured onto a cloth held on the site.

» Place stones or metal objects on the manifold of your car/boat engine to heat while you are taking the person to a medical centre. When the object is hot, wrap in cloth and apply to the wound area.

» Use a cigarette lighter to heat a metal object, then wrap in cloth and place on the wound.

» Immediate transfer to a medical centre/hospital is a must.

## Cobbler and other catfish (Plotosidae)

A number of species of cobbler and catfish inhabit Australian waters, both coastal and in freshwater rivers and billabongs.

All the various forms have three embedded, serrated venomous spines, one in the front edge of the dorsal fin on their head and the other two at the front of the two pectoral fins. These are disguised with a thin covering of skin tissue and appear to be soft fins. The amount of venom received is directly related to the amount of pressure you place on the individual spine. The spines are also serrated so that they tear your flesh as they withdraw. This assists the absorption of venom, causing instant pain. The venom glands are in the skull. Once the head is removed the body is safe to handle.

'Catties' or cobbler can be more than 2 kilograms in size and the fillets are considered good eating.

## Recognition

They all have an eel-like or forked tail. Five sets of cat whiskers surround their mouth. Micro-scales give the impression of smooth skin. All have the three spikes on their head and side fins. They grow up to 60 centimetres in length.

### Precautions

» When walking in shallows, wear stout footwear and shuffle your feet.
» Take care when sorting the catch of a net and/or removing from a fishing line.
» The venom glands are in the head so removing the head removes the venom.

### Signs and symptoms

» Immediate pain, increasing in intensity for a short time, which may move up the affected limb to the lymph gland. The pain can be mild to severe for several hours, and then subsides to a dull ache after another few hours. They are painful, not deadly.

### Treatment

» Immerse stung area in hot/warm water to ease the pain – very effective.
» Seek medical advice if pain persists.

## Puffer fish, porcupine fish and box fish (Tetraodontidae)

All of these fish have a deadly poison called tetrodotoxin (TTX). *Consider the whole fish, its organs and skin deadly poisonous.* There are about 120 different species worldwide and they are the second most poisonous vertebrate (after the 'golden poison' frog). In addition, all of the puffer fish have strong parrot-beak like teeth. Those of the silver puffer fish (north-west blowfish) are very strong, and a bite can remove large chunks of flesh and probably finger tips.

There are species of puffer fish found all around the Australian coastline.

### Recognition

1. **Puffer fish** are capable of blowing themselves up like a ball. They have slimy skin and do not look like normal 'edible' fish – and they are not! At least four people have died in Australia from eating puffer fish flesh.

2. **Porcupine fish** have large, spiky, spine-covered bodies and will also puff up like a ball in defence. They are extremely poisonous to eat.

3. **Box fish** are also toxic. They are encased in plate-like scales that form a bony, armoured skin.

### Precautions
» Do not eat any part of these fish.
» Take care when removing puffer fish from fishhooks; their spines cause painful wounds and the larger ones can bite off chunks of your flesh.
» Wash hands after handling, as some toxins can be excreted through the skin of these fish.

### Signs and symptoms
» Muscular paralysis, possibly leading to respiratory failure. These symptoms can set in within three minutes of eating the flesh of these fish.
» Numbness of tongue and tingling of the lips, vomiting, general weakness, tightening of the chest, dizziness and collapse.
» Hopefully that's enough to put you off experimenting with these deadly fishes.

### Treatment
» Immediate transfer to a medical centre/hospital or call an ambulance.
» Treat respiratory failure if necessary.
» Induce vomiting.
» This is an extreme medical emergency.

## Sea wasp or box jellyfish
## (*Chironex fleckeri*)

The large box jellyfish or 'sea wasp' is the most dangerous jellyfish in the world. They are a real threat and are an extreme danger to anyone swimming, diving or surfing in northern Australia. More than 60 people have been killed by it in subtropical Australian waters since 1900. Box jellyfish can be found in muddy inshore and/or open waters in northern Australia. They are reportedly found most frequently where fresh water flows into the sea and in very shallow water during the 'wet season' between November and April.

### Recognition

The sea wasp is the largest of the box jellyfish. It has a clear, squarish round topped body, which is sometimes the size of a person's head. Tentacles can trail many metres behind the head and are nearly invisible. Heed all local advice and warning signs posted on beaches. Prevention is better than cure.

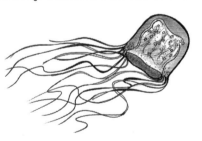

### Precautions
- » Avoid entering the water at any time of the year if these stingers have been reported.
- » You can now wear 'stinger suits' as a form of body protection.

### Signs and symptoms

» Massive local skin destruction - akin to the effect of the lash of a whip.

» Spasm of all muscles, including those of the blood vessels and heart.

» Great pain and shock.

### Treatment

» Speed is important.

» Remove victim from the water.

» Inactivate the nematocysts (stinging cells) with liberal washes with vinegar or lots of Stingose sprayed onto the wounds.

» *Never* use alcohol-based liquids or methylated spirits to neutralise the sting – it makes the nematocysts discharge even more, thus making the sting *worse*, not better.

» After tentacles have been deactivated, remove by using a knife, stick or similar (not your hands).

» Treat for shock and transfer immediately to a medical centre/hospital.

» Although an antivenene is available, the speed and severity of the onset of symptoms can cause death before it can be injected – so act very quickly.

» Better to avoid being stung at all. Read those signs and ask local authorities for advice.

## Bluebottle or Portuguese man-o'-war (*Physalia physalis* species)

The bluebottle is common and well known in our Australian waters for causing painful stings with its blue body and tentacles. No fatalities have been recorded in Australia.

*Recognition*

The bluebottle is not a true jellyfish but is closely related. Their blue float or sail measures 2–15 centimetres, with their blue trailing tentacles being up to 10 metres in length.

*Signs and symptoms*

» Pain is the most prominent feature. The cause of the stinging will appear as localised skin lesions, perhaps with a string of bead-like blue tentacles still attached. Welts will commonly appear.

» Symptoms, apart from a painful stinging sensation, may include headache, nausea and vomiting and abdominal pain.

*Treatment*

Wearing gloves, firstly remove tentacles by washing with sea water and plucking off any remaining, or scrape off with a sharp-edged knife or similar. Do not use vinegar in this instance. New treatment procedures recommend immersion in hot water: 45°C or no hotter than you can tolerate. Soak for a minimum of 20 minutes or pour hot water over the affected area. Heat pads can be applied in the form of hot rocks or water bottles wrapped in cloth.

> » If heat or hot water is not possible, then apply ice or
> ice packs, as this will also alleviate the pain.
> » After the basic first-aid treatment, if there is
> continuing pain or blistering, seek medical advice. A
> topical anaesthetic agent such as a cortisone cream
> may be necessary to reduce the inflammatory reaction.

All other jellyfish stings respond to ice packs and sometimes the accompanying topical anaesthetic cream.

## Blue-ringed octopus
## (*Hapalochlaena maculosa*)

These are found in all shallow areas of the Australian coastline. Their saliva contains a highly toxic venom that is used to paralyse their prey – and which can be fatal to humans. This octopus must bite you with its tiny parrot-like beak, in the centre of its tentacles, to inject the venom into the wound. All bites have occurred out of the water to people accidentally or intentionally handling the little creatures. They use dead shells as their own protected homes and can be found clinging to weeds in rock pools.

*Recognition*

The blue-ringed octopus is small, usually no larger than 12 centimetres across, generally covered with greyish-brown blotches and bands on a wrinkled skin. They can change their colour pattern and texture rapidly to a pattern of small bright iridescent blue rings and small stripes, which appear on the tentacles and body when the octopus is defensively excited.

## Precautions

» Leave any octopus alone that is small and remotely resembles this description!

» Take care when picking up cans and bottles, shells, etc., as these octopuses often make such objects their homes. Do not put items such as dead shells in your pockets, inside your wetsuit or into your wetsuit sleeves.

## Signs and symptoms

» The bite is rarely felt – there may be slight bruising and a spot of blood.

» There may be numbness at the bite site, with difficulty of speech and sight.

» Paralysis may develop rapidly in the person's diaphragm muscle causing respiratory (breathing) difficulty and this can, and has, led to death in Australia.

## Treatment

» *Wash the wound* to remove the venomous saliva, which is usually on the surface at the bite site, then use the pressure immobilisation technique on the affected limb.

» Never leave a (suspected or confirmed) blue-ringed octopus bite victim alone.

» Monitor the victim's breathing – if there is difficulty give mouth-to-mouth resuscitation.

» Constantly check the victim's airway because vomiting is a problem with paralysis – clear any obstruction of the windpipe and place the victim in the recovery position.

» Be aware that the victim may be fully conscious even if paralysed. Reassure them that they won't be left alone, and explain what is happening.

» Keep up ongoing mouth-to-mouth resuscitation until they can breathe again.

» This has been successfully effective in several cases.

» There is no antivenene.

» Seek medical assistance urgently.

## Cone shells (Conoidea)

All cone shells are venomous to some degree and a few can be harmful or deadly. They all have the ability to inject venom with a 'dart' from their proboscis, the trunk-like tube at the front of their shell. They use this appendage to spear fish for food and to protect themselves from predators. Even small cones can deliver venom, so treat all with respect. Cones shells known to be dangerous are distributed all along the Australian coastline.

The geographer cone (*Conus geographus*) I believe is the most deadly one known in the tropical waters of Australia.

### Recognition

Cone shells are cone-shaped marine molluscs (shells). Australian cones vary considerably in shape and size – from a few millimetres to over 10 centimetres.

They are commonly found on rocky reefs, often hidden in the sand or under loose rocks and coral slabs. Others sit on top of the reef and are easily seen. Most have a covering that camouflages them quite effectively, so they are best recognised by their shape.

### Precautions

As the cone shell's proboscis can reach the entire length of its shell or longer, it is *not even safe to pick one up from the 'blunt' end or 'shoulder' of the shell*. Therefore, do not handle cones at all. The dart can penetrate through gloves. They can also penetrate 3-millimetre wetsuits. I met a guy in Exmouth who was stung on the buttocks through his mesh dive bag – his wife saved his life because she recognised the symptoms and drove him straight to the local hospital.

### Signs and symptoms

» Numbness or tingling sensation in stung area.
» Pain and redness plus swelling of area.
» Vomiting.
» Difficulty in breathing, swallowing and visual focusing.
» Death due to respiratory failure can occur.

## Sea snakes (Hydrophiinae)

It is possible that you may encounter a sea snake when you are scuba diving, snorkelling or fossicking in shallow waters or mangrove swamps. Occasionally live snakes can be stranded on the beach after a storm. Call a snake handler to relocate back into the sea or you can help a stranded snake back into the water by using long poles, as they are sluggish on land. When diving, sea snakes are often fearlessly inquisitive, and appear to be aggressive when in fact they are just looking.

Their venom is potent as it must paralyse its fish prey instantly – if the fish swims away there is no scent trail to follow, unlike animals bitten by snakes on land. It is a fallacy that they can't open their mouths up very wide – they can bite any part of your body. Although they are venomous and can bite us humans, they generally require a lot of provocation.

*Recognition*
Their most obvious feature is a flattened, paddle-shaped tail, which is an adaptation to their aquatic lifestyle. Their skin has scales but is not slimy like that of an eel. Sea

snakes are air-breathers like their land-dwelling cousins; their nostrils point upward, rather than forward, and have flaps that close when submerged.

Sea snakes are most common in the tropics, but the Yellow Bellied variety is found in southern waters.

### Precautions

If diving, gently push the snake away. If it is persistent, leave the area or water. They sometimes become mesmerised by their own mirror reflection in your face mask, so look away as you swim away. When I did a stint as a pearl diver I could get them to go away by disturbing the ocean floor with my fin or hand. They would disappear onto the sand/silt looking for food as they thought it was two fishes fighting – a good trick.

### Signs and symptoms
» Same as for a land snake bite: pressure and immobilisation and transport victim to a medical centre/ hospital immediately.
» An antivenene is available.

## Poisonous crabs (xanthid crabs, belonging to the family *Xanthidae*)

Most of the known poisonous crabs belong to this family. They are all small crabs and have a poison similar to the puffer fish, with the same reaction if eaten – very harmful to deadly. *Note:* The poison or toxin is *not* destroyed by cooking or boiling.

## Sharks

People do suffer from shark attacks each year in our waters and on average there is one death per year – so heed this advice but do not be paranoid.

We have heaps of varieties of sharks around Australia and several in our rivers. Any shark can be considered dangerous so leave the water if one is present.

The two main culprits for attacks in our oceans are great whites and tiger sharks, with the bull shark present and dangerous in only a few rivers.

There are some common shark habits that we can take notice of and thereby greatly lessen the chances of an attack. Sharks mainly feed from sunset till dawn and love to eat seals and slower moving large fish, with a trace of blood in the water triggering a feeding attack.

» Don't swim with seals or in their vicinity.
» Avoid swimming or surfing late evening, at night or just on sunrise.
» When spearfishing, never tow dead fish behind you.
» If bleeding, leave the water immediately or don't enter the water.
» Leave the water immediately you hear a shark alarm – which is a siren.
» These sirens are also on shark spotter planes and choppers patrolling the more popular beaches.
» Seek local advice on good swimming places and swim between the flags provided by surf lifesaving clubs at popular beaches.

## Crocodiles

We have two types of crocodiles in Australia: the Johnston's freshwater and the estuarine or saltwater crocodile. They are found from Mackay on the east coast to Coral Bay on the west coast.

### Johnston's croc ('Freshie')

Freshies are found in fresh water and can grow to 3 metres. They live on a diet of fish and will also grab birds, mammals and reptiles, usually on the water's edge. They have rarely attacked people, except for the occasional defensive bite when people tread on them. They are not aggressive by nature and we are too large to be on the menu. They are easily distinguishable from the salties by their longer and narrower snout, with uniform sized teeth. They can be seen in the same areas as the larger aggressive salties but never in the ocean. Treat large freshies with the same respect as you should a saltwater croc.

## Saltwater or estuarine crocodile
## ('salty', 'cheeky one' or 'hand bag')

These animals have a broad solid head and uneven teeth that vary in size. These guys are the really dangerous in their own right and you should never, ever take chances swimming where these creatures live.

They can grow to 6 metres or more and are aggressive hunters and aggressive defenders of their territory. Even though the name 'salty' wrongly suggests they live in salt water they can be found in totally freshwater rivers, large creeks, billabongs and swamps more than 100 kilometres inland from the ocean.

They are very present in river estuaries, ocean beaches and in the waters around offshore islands as well, and have killed people who were snorkelling.

How do you know if they are present in a waterhole or in the ocean in the tropics of Australia? Answer – it is impossible to tell just by looking because they are so well camouflaged and are masters in hunting by stealth. Only by asking sensible locals, National Parks Services, tour operators or the tourist information centres in the area you are visiting will you find out.

Salties have a similar diet to freshies but on a much larger scale – they will grab cattle, horses and people who enter their domain.

In 2005 Dan Duncan and his friend Sonya went out from Kununurra to the Pentecost River for a fishing trip.

On night one after a successful days fishing, they set up their mozzie dome tent 20 metres back from the water's edge, which had a steep mud embankment they thought a croc couldn't or wouldn't climb. At about 3 a.m. they were woken by a pole near their tent falling down. Dan thought it must be the wind blowing it over and had curled his legs up under their new feather-down doona. Then snap! A 4 metre Salty smashed its jaws down on the corner portion of their dome tent and rolled over several times, engulfing them both in a tangled mess in total darkness. With Sonja screaming as the croc was tugging them towards the muddy decline, Dan was able to find and undo the main zipped opening. Sonya escaped as the croc rolled back the opposite direction, now winding tightly on Dan's hand and forearm, so tight that he was now trapped inside the tent. The croc then thrashed its head from side to side, throwing the tent and Dan around like a rag doll. The monster then moved backwards towards the water's edge with powerful half-metre tugs. This continued for at least five minutes. Sonja, now safely in the car, found and connected a hand held spotlight. Yelling for Dan as she searched for him with the powerful light, she saw him still struggling to free himself as the last part of the tent disappeared over into the mud decline. Now 2 metres from the river Dan could hear the running water and knew what the croc had in mind.

The croc, now on the water's edge, rolled several times in the opposite direction, which freed Dan's trapped limb and he was able to escape. Looking back wasn't an option in his mind as he scrambled to freedom, the croc still thrashing the tent and doona in its jaws.

In the car together trying to rest and wait till full sunlight to pack up when they realised the ignition key was still on. The car battery's energy had completely died – dead flat. They were now stranded in a very precarious position.

Dan tried the bush mechanics tricks of spinning the jacked-up back wheel to start the car – didn't work. Push start was impossible as they were parked on sand. He then tried warming the battery near the fire – didn't work. Waited a full day for battery to recharge itself – didn't work.

Dan had been a participant on one of my survival courses in Kununurra only months prior to this. After two more days of being stranded past, with the ever-present danger of the croc returning, he made a plan to walk out to the main Gibb River road and set up a tripod of sticks with a help note. This was the wet season and only a handful of vehicles would use that dirt road a week but someone would eventually find it. He set up the tripod with a detailed note and a request for assistance. He secured the note in a waterproof plastic bag and, with large sets of arrows made of wood and stone, laid out on the tracks indicating the exact route back to their camp. This worked and the occupants of a vehicle from Home Valley Station responded to the note. The occupants said without the arrows on the ground they would have not found the stranded couple. They drove in the 6 kilometres and jump started Dan and Sonja's vehicle. They then retrieved the tent, which was snagged on tree roots with the croc's teeth marks well imbedded in the ripped tent. The doona was gone.

Never underestimate a croc's ability and agility out of water. Fifty metres is the recommended minimum distance you should camp from croc waters. I prefer hundreds of metres away – where I can sleep much more peacefully.

## Crocodile precautions

» Seek out information from reliable sources before you enter their areas.

» Heed all warning signs and the advice of local authorities.

» Common sense is your best guide.

» Don't swim where crocodiles live. (If you swim knowing salties are present you are a bloody idiot.)

» Fish from up a steep-sided bank or rocks a few metres higher than the water level.

» Never fish standing on logs as salties can leap out of the water to ambush you.

» When collecting water take a bucket with a wire handle on it and quickly scoop up the water, then leave the water's edge straight away. Do not go back to the same place twice to refill any water container as crocs could be lying in wait for you.

» Avoid livestock and wildlife drinking spots for the same reason.

» When in a boat, don't dangle arms and/or legs over the sides.

» Crocs leave slide marks when entering the water from their basking spots – avoid these areas as the crocs usually return to these favourite places.

» Don't go near or disturb croc egg nesting sites as the female lies close to protect her eggs and will not hesitate to attack you.

» Don't feed crocodiles. This is a very dangerous practice.

» Clean fish well away from the water's edge and dispose of the fish filleting by-products by throwing them back into deep water.

» Be especially careful during the September–April breeding season. Crocodiles are often more aggressive, territorial and hungry during this time of the year.

» Beware: crocs will follow in a thrashing fish caught on your line. This I have witnessed.

» Set up a camp well above the high-water mark and a minimum 50 metres from the water's edge in croc country, preferably in an area that crocs can't climb up to.

» Many locals opt to sleep on their modified roof racks or in the trayback of their vehicles – not a bad idea.

NOTE: When fishing it is generally good practice, especially in a remote area where assistance is often far away, to simply cut the line and let any of the dangerous fish listed in these notes swim away. The hook will eventually rust away, leaving the fish with no permanent injury, and a potential problem for you will have been averted. For safety and environmental reasons, *stainless steel hooks should never be used.*

## Chapter 16
# SURVIVING IN THE DESERT

Find yourself stranded with little or no water in a desert and you will find yourself in trouble. Deserts are among the harshest environments on earth, with an unforgiving temperament and no tolerance for fools.

### Five mistakes that could prove fatal in the desert

**1:** Not knowing how much water we actually require, per day, every day – which is a minimum of 1 litre per 25 kilograms of body weight.

**2:** Not knowing that sipping your water does *not* prevent dehydration, because a sip amount of water is mainly used up firstly by digestion, and what little remains is then absorbed by your thirsty kidneys and liver – leaving little or no water to hydrate your brain. This is the start of dehydration: it causes headaches, nausea and the loss of your ability to think and perform tasks to the best of your ability.

**3:** Do not run in a desert unless something is chasing you. Do not climb cliffs, slide down scree slopes or jump off anything (as depicted in some reality TV shows), because you do not have a film crew, a chopper or a medic on hand.

**4:** Anyone eating scorpions or spiders risks a possible painful sting, bite or health problems. That action = stupidity.

**5:** '"Glare blindness" only happens in snow.' False: It can happen in deserts too, causing painful and debilitating stress to your eyes. This can result in temporary blindness. It is preventable by wearing a wide-brimmed hat and sunglasses to reduce glare. If you don't have sunglasses you can improvise:

» Stick adhesive plasters on the front of spectacles, leaving just a narrow slit to, limit the amount of light entering the eyes.

» Make glare goggles out of firm paper or thin cardboard by cutting out the shape of a large pair of sunglasses with slits to see through and tying some string on to hold it in place.

» Reduce glare by rubbing charcoal on your cheeks and under your eyes.

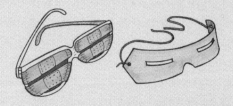

# 'SURVIVAL EYES'

I have spoken a lot about facts and figures in many of the chapters. Most of it is common sense, but the real value of many of these physical bushcraft/survival skills comes into play when our battery-operated high-tech machines fail, get damaged or lost, or run out of energy.

Not so obvious are higher skills a true survivalist should possess. This is the ability to identify and become conscious of what you actually are looking at by making that all-encompassing. Employ and embrace all your other senses, including intuition. This develops the ability to be able to 'read' what you see and what you feel about the environment, enabling you to predict what and where will produce the best results for your endeavours. It helps if you know the best times and places to forage, make or find water, the routes to walk, and when to just stop, wait and think. This is what I call having 'survival eyes'.

My apprenticeship started decades before, in the 1980s, but I didn't know that at the time. It was when I first met these traditional bush men and women of the desert that I realised how good a person could be at staying alive with no outside help or any modern tools. My first Western Australia Museum expedition took seven weeks travelling through the desert, with no roads and no communication to the outside world and no backup of any sort. Therefore our safety officer in charge was 'common sense'. We had seven traditional male elders who were effectively our 'map' to guide us to their traditional habitation and ceremonial sites. At some of these special sites we had to go through ceremonies just to be allowed near them, as I was a non-initiated man – I was 27 years old at the time.

I had talented teachers in these very wise old elders, some of whom did not speak English. Lessons were in knowing edible and medicinal plants and the elders who shared their unbelievable tracking ability. When I started to show signs of ability in these fields they introduced me to the power of observation – putting all of what's around you together, most importantly animal behaviours. Then to turn these observations into strategies of how, where and when to hunt or forage, and when not to waste your time and energy. In other words, how to stay alive and conduct yourselves in the wilderness respectfully.

A young Aboriginal boy was dragging a stick, disturbing the soil. When his grandfather said 'Don't do that', the reply was, 'It is only the soil, it is nothing'. The elder stopped walking and said 'My grandson, everything is something, nothing is nothing'. He had an understanding of the micro world of the soil and its connectedness to all.

So-called reality programs sensationalise a daring act, or eating something venomous or revolting is portrayed as being survivalist. But that is not the true way to behave or act. Many of these reality acts are disrespectful and potentially dangerous – the very opposite of reality.

Even under the stress of a real survival situation there is no need to be discourteous to anyone or aggressive towards the environment. What you give out is what you get back.

Our personal lives and/or wilderness survival are not about having the best hand in the card game. It is really about making the most of what you have been dealt.

Less emotional and more rational responses – that is the answer to most of our problems. It is an essential ingredient for survival in any environment.

The more you know, the less you fear; less time spent in fear means you have more time to think and enjoy your surroundings. In your spare 'mind time' create some time to include the 'care' of your spirit in your daily actions. This is a common thread among traditional peoples.

# Chapter 17

# FINDING YOUR WAY
## with the sun, moon and stars

Our closest star, the sun, and the moon always rise in the east and set in the west. These, plus the star constellations of the Southern Cross and Orion, can be used to find a direction or to navigate by.

## USING THE SUN

Find an open area and place a stick about a metre high firmly in the ground. (A longer stick may possibly lean over to one side with its own weight or be moved by a strong breeze; any movement will give you a false end result.)

Make sure it has a neat top end – not a 'stag-horn' arrangement.

Mark the end of the shadow that it has now created, using a small stick pushed into the ground.

Wait 15 minutes and during that time (if using a 1-metre-high stick) the shadow will move several centimetres. Now place another small stick into the ground at the end of this second shadow.

Now place the toe of your left foot on the first shadow marker peg and the toe of your right foot on the second peg and no matter where in the world you are, you are now facing north.

If the sun is north of you the main upright stick will be in front of you, and it will be behind you if the sun is south of you. It doesn't make any difference: you are still facing north.

## Shadow stick method

Orientating oneself to north is a good idea just to establish where you are in relationship to everything around you. Once you are facing north you can then work out all of your other compass directions. I use another stick placed along the line drawn between the two little markers and that gives me the east–west line. I then form a right angle with a second stick for the north–south directions. When I do this at night I split these sticks with my knife to reveal the white or creamy interior, which is more easily seen in the dark. Using straight sticks at right angles gives you the most accurate improvised compass. Now scribe in N, E, S, W points at the appropriate end of each stick. This will help to orientate you if you are disorientated and lessen the chances of making an error, in what could already be a stressed state of mind.

To convert these crossed sticks accurately into a 360-degree improvised compass, divide each 90-degree section into smaller increments. Then you can choose any direction you require, not just the main compass points. The accuracy of this method can vary, depending where the sun is in relation to your position on earth, so 'aim off' to find your target, particularly if it is a small target.

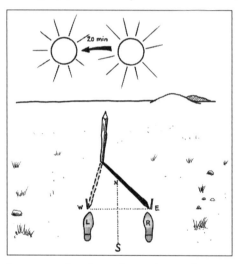

Apart from navigating, knowing where you are in relation to which way the sun moves helps you set up your base camp or tent in the direction that suits you, for example facing your tent away from the early morning sun, or taking account of the movement of shadows so as to set the most shade on your tent, vehicle or gear. It will also help when selecting the best branch to place a plastic bag on for maximum sunlight in the transpiration water-procurement method.

# IN THE TROPICS

Each year the sun moves from the Tropic of Cancer in the north to the Tropic of Capricorn in the south. This movement begins on 21 June and takes six months to complete, so the sun arrives at the Tropic of Capricorn (23.5 degrees south latitude) on 21 December, creating the summer solstice. This is close to Christmas Day every year, making it easier to remember.

You need to remember this because if you are in a tropical zone the sun may be north or south of your location depending on the time of year.

If you don't know where the sun position is in relation to your location, then use a shadow stick to determine this because this will always find north.

Knowing if the sun is north or south of you is relevant to you not becoming disorientated, particularly in a flat wilderness area where you don't have any visual physical features to guide you. If you think the sun is north of you when it is actually south of you, you could become really lost.

## The moon shadow stick

I discovered this technique several years ago while discussing the moon's movements with my friend Ian Lancaster, an ex-USAF navigator.

Our moon is equatorial, which means it goes around the equator, and it too rises east and sets west. When we have enough moonlight for a shadow we can use the shadow-stick method, as we did with the sun, to find north and, consequently, all the other directions. You should know what hemisphere you are in (I hope). And it will be no surprise that when you are in the southern hemisphere the main stick will always be in front of you, and behind you when in the northern half of our world.

This technique is consistently more accurate than the sun because the moon is always going around the equator.

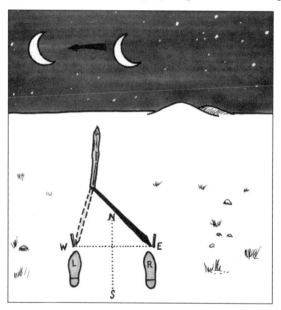

## Using the stars

Before we start, I appreciate that the earth rotates and the stars are fixed but for the purpose of explanation let's talk simply – because we are talking about surviving and not putting lives at risk by any technical confusion.

All the star's positions in the sky are set and they all rotate every night in the exact same relationship to one another. What changes each night is the time that they appear. This time difference alters their position slightly every night, which leads to a completely different location every month over a year. They will appear in the exact same position in the sky at the exact same local time 12 months later.

Our next consideration is that all the stars constantly move at 15 degrees every hour during the night, always in an east to west direction.

There are many methods that can be used to find a direction but some are not too accurate and some are too complicated to remember easily. I have chosen the best two and hopefully you are already familiar with these.

Both these methods apply throughout the southern hemisphere, not just in Australia.

## 1. The Southern Cross

This constellation can only be seen when you are facing in a southerly direction. It consists of four bright stars forming a nearly perfect crucifix (cross) with a smaller star in one bottom quadrant. It can be seen from as far north as Indonesia in the southern hemisphere and is sometimes referred to as the Crux.

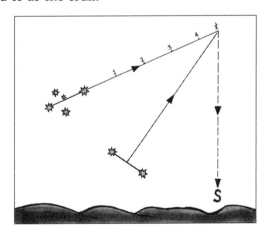

To find south, draw an imaginary line through the long axis of the cross. Extend that four and a half times the length of the cross itself and that location in the sky is called the South Celestial Pole (SCP). There will be no other visible stars close by. Drop that line straight down to the ground and that is south and, if done precisely, you can be within one degree of accuracy of true south.

There are two bright stars associated with the Southern Cross; they are known as the 'Pointers' because they point towards the 'Cross'. If you can recognise these two stars then they can also help you to find the SCP. Draw an imaginary line bisecting the Pointers and note the points where that line intersects the long axis line from the Cross – this gives you the SCP. Drop that position to the ground for south. Again, this is very accurate.

## 2. Orion

This constellation is also known in Australia as the Saucepan, the Pot and more recently the Shopping Trolley.

This set of stars can only be seen when facing north while you are in the southern hemisphere.

To find north, draw an imaginary line through the handle of the Saucepan and through the middle star of the three vertical stars and continue that unbroken line to the ground. This gives you a fairly accurate north point.

This is only accurate when Orion is high in the sky. To be most accurate, when you are looking up, Orion's position should be between 10 and 2 on an imaginary clock face.

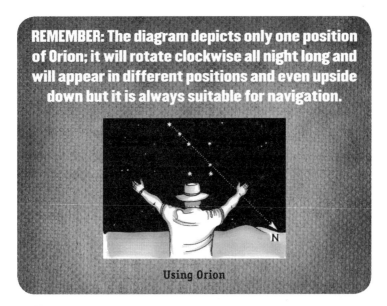

**Using Orion**

## Follow your star

Once I have established the direction I need to travel in, I require something to aim at. Best choice is a star low on the horizon that is in line with my direction. I will gather my two sticks and head off, walking in a straight line towards that star. After 20 minutes I need to recheck that the star hasn't moved too far off-line, remembering that stars move at 15 degrees an hour and will eventually lead me astray.

To recalculate, choose another star and move off again. If there is no star available, then I choose the silhouette of a fixed object that is on the correct line of my direction and head towards that, and so on, until I reach my objective.

## Night vision

Night vision is achieved only after our eyes have not been exposed to any artificial white light for 30 minutes. After that period of time our pupils open as wide as they physically can to capture as much star and/or moonlight as possible. This enables us to see remarkably well in the dark, especially on a moonlit night. This is an advantage to a survivalist who chooses to walk at night out of the heat or to make up time. Even with no moonlight and on a cloudy night we can see at least 20 per cent of what we can during daylight. Using night vision preserves your torch batteries for when you really need them.

Interestingly, we can only see in black and white and not in colour when experiencing night vision.

When walking with night vision 'feel with your feet' – do not place pressure on the ground until you know it is solid. When moving through wooded areas use your hand held up in front of your face to prevent your eyes or face from being injured from unseen sticks.

The colour red does not impede your night vision so use a red-coloured filter lens (if you have one – red lenses are supplied with many pencil torches) over your torch if you wish to retain your night vision. I have used a red light many times but it makes depth perception difficult and reading a coloured map is nearly impossible. I now sacrifice my night vision to do any map reading and use a low-level white light while keeping one eye closed. If you are in a group then get the path finder to close their eyes and turn their back on the offending white light to retain their good night-seeing power. It makes a massive difference.

## Time, or watch, method

I prefer to call this technique the 'time method' because all you need to know is the local time with no daylight saving applied. You can use your analog or digital watch, the radio-broadcast time or the time display in your vehicle or on your mobile phone.

Establish your position in relationship with the sun. Is it north or south of you?

**North**

If you are unsure, then use the shadow-stick method to determine this. From then on, you can use the watch method, which saves you time and effort when navigating over a distance.

When the sun is north of you, point (or imagine) the 12 position of your watch directly at the sun, then bisect the angle between the 12 and the hour hand, and that is north.

When the sun is south of you, point the hour hand at the sun and bisect the angle back to the 12 position, then that direction is south.

**South**

Both of these are fairly accurate but I would still advise 'aiming off' to find your target if it is small.

## NAVIGATION HINTS

I have searched for a couple of people who simply got lost while going to the toilet in the bush. The best was a search for a missing person from a backpacking expedition in the Dwellingup forest of Western Australia. He went to the toilet away from his group, who took off their backpacks and lay down to rest. He got disorientated and couldn't see them when he turned around. His ego would not allow him to call out to locate them as he was embarrassed about being 'lost'. He panicked and started to run, looking for them. I found him four hours later, 16 kilometres away and still running in the wrong direction.

Even on my training courses several groups have become 'geographically embarrassed' on their navigation exercises, but that is not so concerning, as they were all together and had been given an emergency direction out of the forest. In the end, most groups took that option and walked back to the base camp unassisted.

Getting lost is always due to human error, in ways too numerous to mention. Most get lost on the last leg of their trip, when they are either tired or overconfident, or both, and not paying attention to detail.

I've noticed that people are usually more accurate when using a compass at night than during the day. Fear of the dark and fear of getting lost at night seems to increase concentration and focus.

» Don't just wander off: use your compass or solar/stellar navigation methods to establish the correct direction to take.

» Always think, talk and walk in compass directions, rather than 'left' and 'right'. For example: I am walking east now to the track, then south to the T-junction, then west – and so on. This enables you to think laterally.

» Write the directions down on a piece of paper and take it with you.

» As you walk, look back regularly to see what the country looks like from that direction. You may need to return that way and this will aid your memory. In dense bush this may be as often as every 50 metres or less.

» If you will be returning by the same route, write down or physically mark with flagging tape any distinctive features. Scrape an arrow with your foot on the ground at all junctions indicating the right way home.

» Convert your compass bearing to a 'back bearing' to go back the way you came. To do this add or subtract 180° and follow that direction home.

» It's important to know the exact distance that you need to travel, and keep a record of the distance travelled as you go, either by time, or more accurately by 'pacing'.

# How to 'pace'

» Count your distance – to calculate the distance travelled, convert your paces, or steps, to 100-metre lots. The average person walks at 140 paces per 100 metres. Count your steps and record every 100 metres as a knot on a long piece of string.

» 10 knots = 1 kilometre and so on.

» To make life easier, if you count every time your left foot takes a pace, you only need to count half as much. (70 double paces = 140 paces = 100 metres.)

» For greater accuracy, work out your own paces over a known 100 metres before you go bush.

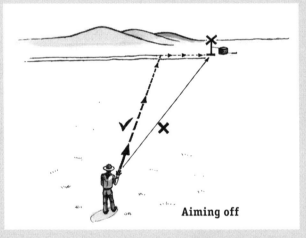

Aiming off

» When using a compass bearing to locate a target which is located on a linear feature like a track, deliberately aim off to one side of it. When you arrive at that track, fence or creek line, turn and walk confidently to your target. This means you may walk an extra few hundred metres but it eliminates the worry of not being precise. It is an excellent navigation aid. A linear feature is also known as a 'catching' feature.

» We all have a tendency to walk to the right or left of every object we come across. We don't walk left, then right, then left, etc. Most people have a right-hand tendency which means that without knowing it, they will curve to the right when trying to walk in a straight line. Some peoples' tendency is so strong that if they walk for long enough they will walk in a complete circle. Even with a compass you must be conscious of not always walking to the right side of every object you choose on your bearing. Over several kilometres this can push you off-target by several hundred metres and explains why individuals and groups can get lost while navigating with a compass and map.

» If you come across an obstacle that can't be crossed, such as a swamp, lake or rocky outcrop, and your compass points straight ahead, you need to carefully detour around it. Stop on the edge of the obstruction, dial in a 90-degree turn on your compass and walk alongside the obstruction, counting your paces as you go. When you are clear of the obstruction, stop. Dial up your original bearing and continue past the obstruction and add that distance onto your original route distance. Once past the obstruction, dial up the 'back bearing' of your detour and walk along the other side of the obstruction for the same number of paces of the first detour. This should have you clear of the obstruction and back onto your original bearing. Stop and dial up your original bearing and continue on.

 OWL WISDOM: **Make life easier by thinking and talking in directions when in the bush and 'aim off' to find your target when you can.**

# Chapter 18
# KIDS IN THE BUSH

Young children should have a few 'survival items' in their little day packs for every venture – particularly in large bush areas where the inquisitiveness and wonder of your child's mind should be encouraged, with their safety being paramount at all times. You can start by dressing them in brightly coloured clothes, especially their hat, which should be an easy-to-see fluoro colour. Another good idea is to attach little bells onto a toddler's clothing so parents can tell where the little one is at all times.

## A USEFUL DAY PACK FOR KIDS

Children's day-pack items should include:

- » Tissues
- » Lollies
- » Whistle
- » LED Torch

- » Favourite toy
- » Lightweight jacket
- » Brightly coloured poncho-style raincoat
- » Water and spare juice drink
- » Colouring-in book and pencils

## Make friends with a tree

If lost, these young ones should be encouraged to make friends with a tree, a 'friendly tree', and stay there. Show them a large tree in an open area as an example, and make it a protective area, not a scary one. Usually anything taller is a threat in young minds so reinforce the safety of this 'friendly tree'. Sit with them, staying in the shaded area, and explain why this is important. Look for interesting features on the tree that give it character and give the tree a name.

- » They should never lose sight of their new 'friend'. They can use its shade when hot or for cover from wind or rain.
- » They can hang their tissues as high as possible in a circle around the tree as a signal.
- » If they blow their whistle three times every few minutes it will help them to be found.
- » They can use their colouring book (or some other mind-occupying game) while at the friendly tree.
- » Definitely no fire lighting – this is dangerous.
- » Show them how to use their torch.
- » Demonstrate the correct use of the rain poncho for warmth/shelter and how to use it as a signalling device.
- » Play an 'I am lost' game as rehearsal prior to excursions or camping.

## Make a poncho

It can be fun to make this before going on an excursion. Cut head and arm holes in an orange bin liner to fit your child. (These holes also decrease the danger of suffocation.)

## Teenagers

High school age means they are now young adults and should be treated as such. They are responsible for themselves to a degree and should be encouraged to make their own more comprehensive emergency bush-survival kit, small enough to carry on all outings and in any mode of transport.

Make practising techniques interesting and enjoyable. Lead by example – get stuck into learning yourself and have fun with them.

» Learn the basics of the Big 5 Priorities for wilderness survival.
» Add the trilogy items for survival. That is: their survival kit combined with a rescue blanket and three snake bite bandages per person will ensure maximum safety.
» Again, be careful of fire-lighting techniques with teenagers – include accountability and responsibility.
» Encourage water management practices, and teach procurement and purifying methods.

# Chapter 19
# AUSTRALIAN SNAKES

Snakes are really misunderstood in Australia – most people demonise them to the point of uncontrolled fear through to phobias.

I do understand that they are not very high up on the 'cuddle factor' but do we need to fear them to the point of killing them all?

In Australia we have around 170 species of snakes including sea snakes and burrowing snakes.

Of these only 30 are considered to have life-threatening venom. Fortunately for all of us these all belong to one group of snakes known as elapids, meaning they have fixed front fangs. Being fixed and not hinged means they are not long. The average length would be 4–6 millimetres on a metre long snake and up to 12 millimetres on a very large snake.

We have around 2000 to 3000 people bitten each year and on average we have one death a year from snake bite in Australia.

# TREATMENT FOR SNAKE BITE

The most frequently asked question is 'How long does it take for the venom to react once someone is bitten?' Very hard question to answer because there are many ingredients that vary greatly to contribute to the answer, including the type and amount of venom injected, the person's health, age and possible allergic reaction to that type of venom.

The most venomous and dangerous snake in the world is the one that is in front of you at the time.

# TREATMENT METHOD

I believe the pressure and immobilisation technique (PIT) is the most effective first-aid treatment for all venomous land and sea snake bites in Australia and other elapid snakes worldwide. As a person who has been teaching venomous snake handling courses professionally for more than ten years I thoroughly endorse this method.

To my knowledge there have been no reported deaths once this bandaging has been applied.

The short fangs of the elapid snakes deliver the venom into our lymphatic system and not directly into our blood stream. The venom can only go systemic (enter your body's blood flow and then reach organs) via our lymph glands, which are in our armpits and groin. These glands filter out and combat any foreign material introduced though a cut, wound or bite. Your lymphatic system doesn't have a 'pump' – it is your muscle movement now that will pump the venom into your system. Immobilisation is as critical as pressure.

The bandaging slows the venom movement and absorption rate down to as much as one twentieth, buying the victim much more time to get to a hospital. The slower rate of absorption allows your body's immune system time to contest the venom by producing its own form of 'anti-venom' resistance.

## Step 1: 'Calm Down'

Sit the person down in a comfortable and safe position. Stay calm and reassure the victim that this bandaging will arrest the venom's movement to a trickle, and they will not die. Do not try and catch the snake as it is not necessary for ID – you are wasting precious first-aid time and someone else may get bitten. Phone/radio for an ambulance or medical evacuation now. It is better if you can let the victim use the mobile/satellite phone or radio while you commence the first aid because it is imperative that the pressure bandages are applied ASAP.

## Step 2. 'Apply Pressure Bandage'

For an arm or hand bite, firstly remove their watch and any jewellery; bitten on the leg, remove boot and sock. Do not remove their shirt or trousers as this excessive movement will increase the absorption and circulation of the venom. You can effectively bandage over their clothing if necessary, applying the same firm pressure you would for a sprained knee/ankle injury. The pressure of the bandage should be tight enough for you to be able to push (not slide) one finger underneath the wrapping. Each bandage wrap should cover 50 per cent of the width of the previous wrap. Start about 20 centimetres *above* the bite site and bandage *down* the limb with the first bandage.

Leave the toes or fingers exposed so that you can monitor the patient's blood circulation later.

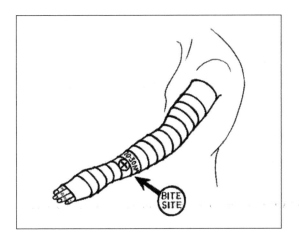

The *second* bandage starts where the first bandage started but this time bandage *up* the arm or leg. On an adult leg you may require the *third* bandage to reach their groin area; on an arm, keep wrapping up to the arm pit.

Once the entire bitten limb is bandaged, check the victim's blood circulation by gently squeezing the blood out of an exposed finger or toe. The skin colour should return within four seconds – meaning you have *not* cut off the circulation in the bandaged limb. If the colour does not return or the victim is saying the bandage is now painful then slowly remove the bandages (one at a time) and replace with the correct pressure.

## Step 3. 'Call for help'

If you haven't been able to previously, call for help now. In Australia dial 000 and ask for an ambulance, or in remote areas for the RFDS or a rescue team.

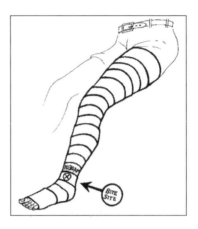

## Step 4. 'Mark the bite site location'

This is important: use a pen to circle the bite site area and write 'bite site' and the time. No pen? Then improvise with charcoal or spit and dirt rubbed onto the bandage. Ask the victim if they have any known allergies and get the contact details of the victim's doctor or family and write that info onto the bandaging as well. Some patients faint or collapse en route to a medical facility. Include your name and contact number on the bandaging in case the hospital staff or medics need extra information you may have. Any of that information could help save a life.

The hospital staff will cut open the marked 'bite site' bandaged area and swab the skin at that site to retrieve a trace of venom. This trace is what they use to positively ID the type of snake that bit the person.

## Step 5. 'Immobilise the limb'

Immobilise the limb by either using a splint, or by bandaging the feet together or bandaging the hand onto the victim's leg whilst in a sitting position. Limit the patient's movements. Move the patient by carrying them, or have transport come to them. They can walk a short distance with a bandaged arm slung low. Never walk on a bandaged leg because the strong leg muscles will pump the venom into your system easily making the PIT treatment only 10 per cent effective.

## Treatment for bites to a person's body, neck or face

Immediately apply pressure over the bite site using their or your hand. Where possible use a bandage but do not restrict chest movement. Seek medical help immediately and keep the pressure on the bite site at all times. Remember to keep the patient's physical movement as limited as possible.

**DO NOT:**
Wash the bite site
Use a tourniquet
Elevate the limb
Apply an ice pack
Attempt to catch the snake
Try and suck out the venom

In hospital the staff will treat the reactions or symptoms of the venom in the patient, with only 10 per cent of all snake bite cases requiring antivenene. Some people's allergic reactions to the antivenin can be more life-threatening than the original snake venom. So don't get bitten.

## Lack of knowledge

Many people don't understand the difference between the bite site *signs* and snake bite *symptoms*. The life-threatening symptoms will not be felt until the venom has travelled from the bite site and entered your body via your lymph glands when you have been bitten on a limb.

Signs of a bite can include fang marks, which may be a distinct double puncture mark, scratch-type marks or multiple punctures. Some excess venom may be visible on the skin. There may be bruising with oozing blood, swelling and numbness, but sometimes no obvious visual indications of a bite and envenomation can be seen, and there is often no stinging or burning sensation.

In the past there have been some serious mistakes from people who went into denial about the seriousness of the bite because of the lack of these signs. They continued moving about with no treatment until the venom went systemic and the ill effects started. By that time starting basic first aid can be too late, but PIT should still be applied to slow down further absorption of the remaining venom.

**Treat all bites as serious.** Immediately apply the bandaging method and call for an ambulance or an alternative medical evacuation to the nearest medical centre, or preferably a hospital.

Improvised bandages can be made from any clothing but stretch materials such as T-shirts are best. Remember to cut them into 10-centimetre-wide strips.

## Symptoms

Serious symptoms will develop once the venom enters a person's system, affecting organs and vital functions. They include:

» blurred vision

» abdominal pain

» headache

» nausea, vomiting

» irritability, confusion

» blood-coloured urine

» painful, tender muscles

» shock, collapse, unconsciousness

» difficulty in breathing to respiratory failure

## Prevention is better than cure

» Do not approach a snake: it doesn't know what your intention is, and that you are just observing or trying to help it.

» Do not cast your shadow onto a snake, as that will also make it nervous.

» You can make a snake very scared by pointing and waving your arms in the air above the snake, so instead, keep your movements calm and slow. Also, don't raise your feet up in front of the snake – that will provoke a strike.

» Wear closed-in footwear at all times when bushwalking and preferably wear long trousers and/or gaiters.

» Use a dead stick or your walking stick to probe long grass as you walk through, as this will encourage the snake to move out of your path.

» Snakes' actions are much, much faster than our reactions, so do not try to touch or catch them unless you have been formally taught and have the correct gear with you.

» Walk slowly away from or move slowly around snakes – don't confront them.

» If a snake visits your shed or home call a qualified snake removalist to deal with it.

» When bushwalking, always take your snake bite bandages.

» Important: practise the pressure and immobilisation bandaging technique before 'reality bites'.

 **OWL WISDOM: The most dangerous snake in Australia is the one that has hold of your leg at the time. Leave snakes alone.**

# Chapter 20
# BITES AND STINGS

Australia is often referred to as one of the deadliest places on the planet and has a wide variety of small and large locals that can kill an adult human. An interesting, but scary, thought is that we have in Australia one or more deadly creatures in each category of animal groups on the earth.

Many of the creatures mentioned in this section may cause a severe allergic reaction known as anaphylaxis which can be fatal if not treated immediately.

## What is anaphylaxis?

It is a severe reaction to a protein-based allergen that may be present in insect venoms, medicines, antivenenes and foods. The person usually has a history of this sensitive allergic reaction but in rare cases anaphylaxis can be triggered by the first incident. Untreated, this is life-threatening. The symptoms include:

» Wheezy breathing
» Swelling of tongue and throat

- » Difficulty with speech
- » Upper body tightness
- » Stomach pain, nausea and vomiting
- » Confusion and loss of consciousness or collapse
- » Young children become limp-limbed

If any of these symptoms occurs, it is a medical emergency. *Seek urgent medical attention.*

Lesser but still concerning reactions are:
- » Swelling at sting/bite site
- » Swelling of the face, lips and eyes
- » Running fluid from eyes and nose
- » Hives and/or welts on skin surface
- » Nausea, headache and/or anxiety

All of these symptoms, including the lesser reactions, need to be reported to a medical doctor ASAP for relief treatment with antihistamine tablets or a prescription for an EpiPen.

# WHAT ARE ANTIHISTAMINES?

Histamine is produced by your body's natural defence system and is released when the body reacts to a foreign substance. When this substance enters your body it is known as an *allergen*.

When the allergen is too strong it causes the release of excessive amounts of histamine, which in turn causes a reaction that includes swelling, rashes and itching.

Antihistamines are medicines that can be used to stop histamine from being released in your body. This relieves the severe itching and/or other symptoms.

There are two different types of antihistamine – the older types produce a sedating or drowsiness effect that the more modern drugs don't. They are both equally effective but if you do not want to be drowsy take the newer sort.

Children and pregnant women should not take antihistamines unless prescribed by a doctor.

Antihistamine tablets are available from pharmacies without a prescription, and the pharmacist will be able to recommend one suitable for you. In the rare case of an adverse reaction to the antihistamines seek advice from a doctor.

This is very serious stuff. Before you go remote, check with all members of the group for allergies. If yes, ascertain the details of their symptoms, where their personal medication is stored and how they want that administered if they can't do it for themselves. Ask their permission to administer their medication for them in an emergency.

Knowing how to carry out first aid has save people's lives and will continue to do so, so please at least learn the basics.


# SPIDERS

The vast majority of the 2000 species of spiders in this continent are shy and considered harmless. Only a few will bite when provoked or when they feel threatened.

Like all creatures they have an important role to play in the earth's ecosystem, of which we are also a part.

In my opinion they are an asset around your house as they naturally keep down the numbers of mosquitoes and other insect pests. As with everything and everybody else on this planet, let's co-exist with some respect and harmony. With the more dangerous species, remove and relocate them.

Australia has only two species that are considered to be highly dangerous to humans. These are the funnel-web, the most dangerous spider Aussie, and the redback. Both have a potentially fatal bite.

I would also include the mouse spider species in a list of dangerous spiders. They exist throughout the mainland and Tasmania and are often mistaken for funnel-webs. Treat a bite from these or any other large black spider as you would a funnel-web bite.

## Funnel-web spider
## (belongs to the family Hexathelidae)
The larger females can be 6–7 centimetres long, with the slightly smaller males having venom that is five times more potent. Both are black in colour and possess large

fangs powerful enough to penetrate through your fingernail! This spider is mostly found near Sydney, with related species found along the eastern coast, and they have been reported as far north as Brisbane. Again, treat any large black spider bite as potentially life-threatening.

## Redback spider
## (*Latrodectus hasselti*)

The adult female spider is 2–3 centimetres long, black or dark brown, with a distinctive red blotch or wide stripe on its body/abdomen. The male is tiny and considered harmless. Neither is aggressive but there are hundreds of reported bites each year. Fortunately, since the antivenene was developed 40 years ago there have been no recorded deaths. The bite is immediately painful; the pain may involve the whole limb. Sweating at the bite site is common. Full envenomation usually results in headache, nausea, possible vomiting, stomach pain and hypertension. Antivenene is available and reliable, with about 250 people receiving it in Australia annually.

## White-tailed spider
### (*Lampona cylindrata* and *L. murina*)

 These spiders are spread across Australia and are common finds in your mulch, and they are wanderers that do end up inside people's houses.

Their bite causes a stinging sensation but is not life-threatening. They can also cause a rare side-effect of skin and muscle necrosis.

There is no scientific evidence that the venom causes this horrible reaction; it is more than likely caused by fungal bacteria present on their fangs at the time of the bite.

# BEES (*Apis mellifera*)

There is only one bee species in Australia to be wary of and that is the introduced European honey bee. These bees will usually only attack in defence of the hive, or when they are grasped or trodden on. The sting of a honey bee can be painful, but usually causes only local pain and swelling.

Some victims can suffer from the life-threatening reaction known as anaphylactic shock, or anaphylaxis. This is a systemic reaction, making it hard to treat without drugs, and without the appropriate treatment there can be fatal consequences.

Any person with this allergy to bee stings should be well educated in both prevention and self-treatment.

### Removing the sting
Scrape the sting out of the person's skin and dispose of it safely – do not use tweezers or your fingernails, because there is a venom sac attached to the end of the sting, and you will squeeze the remaining venom into the victim.

# WASPS

Wasps are great scavengers. They are usually found around areas of human habitation and activity, and pose a particular hazard: unlike bees, wasps do not die after stinging, and will often sting more than once. Stings usually result in minor symptoms such as localised pain and swelling, but they can be fatal for people who are hypersensitive to the stings of these insects.

### European wasp (*Vespula germanica*)

 This is an introduced species in Australia and has a particularly nasty sting. It likes to live around people because we often supply its preferred foods and sweet drinks. These wasps look like a bee in size and shape, with a bright black and yellow body and long antennae.

## Symptoms
» Can be multiple stings
» Painful burning sensation
» Red coloured lump(s)
» Inflammation at bite site
» Severe allergic reaction can occur, causing anaphylaxis

## Treatment for severe cases
» Use EpiPen if the victim has one
» If not, apply the pressure and immobilisation technique
» If the person is stung on the torso or face apply immediate pressure to that site with your hand
» Call for an ambulance or transport to medical centre immediately
» Treat with the same techniques and call an ambulance or transport to medical centre if a child has been stung more than five times or an adult stung ten times or more.

## Treatment for less severe stings
» Clean affected area with soap and water
» Apply ice or cold pack
» Administer pain-reducing medications and creams if required
» If prolonged swelling or stinging sensations occur, seek antihistamine treatment

## Paper wasps (*Polistes*)

These are the wasps with a thin, paper-like nest. They are totally aggressive when anyone or anything approaches their nest area. Expect dive-bomb attacks with short, painful stings. These are a native wasp with much less chance of a severe reaction but be aware of a rare but present excessive allergic reaction from some people. The treatment for an allergic reaction is the same for as for the European wasp sting.

In Australia our native wasps are less aggressive and have less potent venom. They will still sting but usually need provocation. I don't know of anyone being stung by a native wasp and suffering an allergic reaction, and they have never been a problem in the bush. However, there could be people with allergies to these natives as well, so monitor for reactions.

# ANTS

Many ants have a sting at the tip of their abdomen which they use to inject venom into their victims. Some ants lack stings. Instead they bite and 'spit' formic acid into the wound. In most cases an ant bite or sting causes only a sharp stab of pain for a few minutes. People who are allergic to ant bites or stings, however, will suffer a more serious reaction.

Ant species number around 1300 in Australia. Most common stings are from bull ants, jumper ants and green tree ants.

### Bulldog or bull ants (*Myrmecia* species)

These ants are aggressive and can be as large as 25 millimetres in length, with long, powerful jaws and a venom-laden sting in their tail. They deliver a very painful, jabbing sting and often sting repeatedly until shaken off.

### Treatment
» An ice pack or commercially available 'ice' spray may be used to relieve the pain of the sting.
» If there is evidence of an allergic reaction, medical attention should be sought.
» A bush remedy is to massage bracken fern or pigface juice vigorously into the stinging area to alleviate the pain – this does work. I have used it myself and on several others, from primary school children to adults.

## Jumper ants (*Murmeua pilosula*)

Jumper ants (10–15 millimetres long) are aggressive and, just like bull ants, they use a sting in the tail to administer venom. Known in South Australia as 'hopper ants', they move with a hopping motion and can jump 50 millimetres, hence their most common name. They are found in the south-east and south-west corners of the continent, as well as South Australia, but are most concentrated in Tasmania, where they are considered a real health concern in bushland, due to the vast number of colonies.

These little buggers cause the majority of serious allergic reactions and in some cases trigger anaphylaxis, which has been fatal. Please treat the presence of these ants as extremely dangerous. Beware that even first-time stings can bring on serious reactions that require urgent medical assistance. Monitor all victims for life-threatening reactions and be prepared to take action.

### 1. Symptoms (severe reaction)

» Difficulty with breathing and swelling of the throat area, with difficulty in speech
» Pain in the chest or abdomen with nausea, confusion and collapse – this is a medical emergency.

### Treatment

» As for a bee sting: EpiPen injection delivering adrenaline and urgent transfer to a medical centre.

### 2. Lesser (but still serious) symptoms

» Swelling in face area, hives and/or welts in the immediate sting area, followed by headaches and often anxiety.

### Treatment

» Wash the sting site thoroughly with soap and water.
» Apply a cold pack – this relieves the pain and swelling. Antihistamine tablets are recommended for pain relief.
» If soreness and/or swelling persist seek medical advice.

## Green tree ants or weaver ants (*Oecophylla smaragdina*)

Green tree ants are found only in the northern half of Australia and are 8–10 millimetres long. Their common name gives their description – lime-green in colour, these ants live in trees. *Oecophylla* means 'house leaf' because they weave green leaves together to form their nests or homes.

These ants enthusiastically defend their nests and deliberately drop onto you in numbers if you pass too close under the nest. This I have experienced and it is painful, so be observant and avoid any close encounters with the nests.

They have no sting but deliver a nasty bite with their front pincers, then secrete a form of formic acid into the wound. This causes a sharp stinging sensation and discomfort for a few minutes but nothing more. Wash the bite site and if swelling or irritation persists take antihistamine tablets.

A 'bush beverage' can be made by crushing the green ants' abdomen fluid as a lime juice 'cordial' to sweeten fresh water.

## SCORPIONS (ORDER: Scorpiones)

We have 29 species of scorpions covering all parts of Australia from Tassie to Darwin and ranging in size from 2–12 centimetres. All can deliver a very painful to severe sting but none are considered dangerous. Most are nocturnal but some are active during the day. Remember, Australia has no scorpions that can kill you.

Their venom has no life-threatening effects, even in children. Researchers from the University of Newcastle have found that, while the stings cause severe pain for several hours, they seem to have no major systemic effects. In the 95 case studies of people who had been stung, all experienced immediate localised pain, with

80 per cent experiencing severe pain lasting on average six hours.

 I know about the pain! I have been stung twice. Once while carrying firewood I was stung on my upper arm; the other time I was stung on my finger while gathering paperbark for a plate. It hurts like a hot needle stuck in your skin – then slowly, slowly subsides.

### Treatment

» Apply ice or a cold pack and take antihistamine tablets
» If no ice pack is available then apply heat in the form of a hot-water compress of cloth, or a heated stone wrapped in cloth placed directly onto the bite site to ease the pain
» If pain persists and is not subsiding after a few hours, seek medical aid

### Side-effects

These include redness, tenderness, numbness, nausea, headaches and possible depression.

Interestingly, scorpions glow a pale green/white colour under a UV light.

Most people were stung when they stepped on a scorpion – obviously not wearing any footwear. I reiterate, *always wear covered footwear in the bush.*

# TICKS

Ticks are parasites that feed on animal and human blood. They are present throughout Australia and we only need to be conscious and responsive to the small but irritating effects of their bites (including on pets).

## Paralysis tick (*Ixodes holocyclus*)

This tick is only found in a 30-kilometre wide strip along the eastern coastline of Australia. It secretes a neurotoxin in its saliva that causes a progressive, dangerous allergic reaction in humans that can be fatal, but which these days thankfully is very rare. The female tick has to stay attached to a body for several days to produce the symptoms – a less likely event today due to better medical and public awareness. Antitoxins now available have prevented any deaths from tick paralysis for many decades. A few cases of tick paralysis in children are seen at major hospitals each year. Additionally, ticks take a high toll on pets every summer.

*Symptoms*
» Unsteady gait
» Increased weakness of the limbs
» Multiple rashes
» Headache
» Fever
» Flu-like symptoms
» Tenderness of lymph nodes
» Partial facial paralysis

In some susceptible people tick bites may cause a severe allergic reaction or anaphylactic shock, which can be life threatening.

» If swelling of the face and throat causes breathing difficulties, seek urgent medical attention

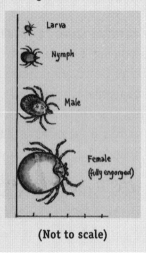

**(Not to scale)**

## Bush ticks (*Ixode* species)

These ticks are present throughout our continent, usually in such low numbers that they raise little or no concern most of the time.

However, there are a few scattered locations where they can be found in large numbers, so heed the advice of locals and don't camp or bushwalk through these infested areas. These places are rare but it is worth asking the question of the locals, information centres or tour guides.

### *Removal and treatment*

Remove a tick as soon as possible after locating it. Use fine-pointed tweezers and grasp the tick as close to the skin as possible. Gently pull head and body straight out with a steady pressure. Don't squeeze too hard on its body as that pressure will force more toxic saliva into your skin – pull firmly up. If the head breaks off then remove as you would a splinter or use a drawing ointment such as Magnoplasm.

Do not try any other method. Old tales of burning them off will only make them excrete their toxins into you. Would you back into a burning cigarette or hot needle? Of course not; neither will they.

Coating them with Vaseline or a dob of liquid soap will make them move, but this could take some time. This is too long to wait, particularly if it is a paralysis tick, and most people want the parasite off them immediately. If you have lots of the larval-stage ticks, often referred to as 'pepper' or 'grass' ticks, which appear as a small, black, pepper-grain-sized dot on top of a lumpy bite site, again remove them using tweezers, or a 30-minute soak in a hot bath with one cup of bicarbonate of soda mixed in will help remove most of them. Follow up with a physical tick inspection and remove any remaining ticks with tweezers.

After the removal of any tick it is really important to massage in some antiseptic solution to help heal the tiny wound and reduce the after-effects of swelling, as well as the terrible irritation of itchiness.

To reduce the itchiness, take a course of non-drowsy antihistamine tablets. You can also alleviate the itching with heat. Take a hot shower or bath, or simply run hot water over the bite sites. This does reduce the pain and itchiness for a few hours.

In the bush you can apply hot rocks wrapped in cloth, or spray with any underarm deodorant — the stinging effect of the acetate in the spray will help ease the itchiness. Deep Heat and other muscle-heating lubricants will also give much relief.

This heat treatment applies for all itching bites from sand flies, mosquitoes, fleas and midges.

### Prevention

Wear a long-sleeved shirt untucked into your pants to let the ticks and anything else fall off. Long trousers tucked into your socks or boots apply for the same reason. Spray your bush clothes and boots with insect repellent prior to entering tick areas.

On return from such areas remove your clothes and place in a dryer, set on hot, for 20 minutes. This will kill any remaining ticks and they won't enter your house. If you leave your bush clobber on the floor or even in a wash basket overnight they will crawl all over the house in search of a new mammal host, with anyone – or any pet – as the target.

## Centipedes (Chilopoda)

Centipedes have somewhere between 15 and 191 pairs of legs – it is always an uneven number. They are found throughout Australia and they do bite with their two powerful front fangs, but none are deadly.

These guys have a mean but not fatal bite. They can be big and their appearance is scary, particularly the larger ones, which are around 20 centimetres long. The two bites I have experienced lasted about two hours, with local intense pain, then subsided quickly.

The first bite was from a little tacker about 50 millimetres long which I thought couldn't inflict a bite through the skin on my fingers – I was wrong.

The second was a large one that somehow got into my mozzie dome and I was awakened at 2 a.m. with a bite to my middle toe – not the sort of alarm clock I would recommend.

The tail end has two menacing long feelers which are completely harmless and are used to grab prey and to ward off their predators.

### Treatment
» Wash bite site and apply ice or a cold pack
» Take antihistamine tablets if symptoms persist

# Chapter 21
# BLISTERS, BOOTS AND CHAFES

It is your feet and your mind that take you to where you want to be in life at any given moment. So please take very good care of both.

During my advanced courses, where people walk 15 to 20 kilometres a day, I have repeatedly witnessed blisters varying from annoying to debilitating. Take blisters seriously and treat them as soon as there is any discomfort rather than ignoring them and suffering the consequences. The trick is prevention by having good socks and broken-in boots prior to any long walk.

It is the movement up and down that creates blisters. Make sure your laces are firmly tightened *all* the way up your boot. For this reason I prefer boots with lace-locking devices halfway up each boot.

If your feet are feeling hot and tired then at every rest

break take off your boots and elevate your feet. This cools your feet and eases the swelling by allowing the blood to drain out of your feet and back into circulation.

Once a 'hot' spot starts, or a blister has developed and you can't tighten your boots comfortably, pull out your laces and cut them in half. Relace and retie off the first half-lace firmly halfway up your boot. Then rethread the other half to the top of the boot and again make firm. This is often all that is needed to stop that blister-causing movement.

If a blister has formed, lance the bottom end and let it drain. This releases the pressure. If you do have Condy's crystals or iodine in your kit, soak the feet in a warm bath with either of these in solution. If not, soak anyway and the warm water will wash out the wound area. Allow feet to dry and the blister to drain before applying a dressing.

If you have a hypodermic needle and syringe, use this to inject a mild antiseptic solution behind the skin. Push the needle through the top layers of dead skin and carefully pump in the solution, and let that drain out a hole in the bottom.

I highly recommend Fixomull or Hypafix brands of plaster. Both are available in small or large rolls from all pharmacies. They provide a thin, breathable, flexible dressing that conforms to the shape of your foot. This stuff is amazing as a wound dressing, used directly over blisters or open wounds to allow healing to occur largely undisturbed. Use either of these to plaster any potential hot spots prior to walking. This is really effective in the prevention of foot blisters.

Hypafix is more easily removed from the wound after use when it has been soaked in water or with a smear of cooking oil applied on top of the dressing plaster itself.

Cover the deflated blister with one layer of Hypafix but never cut off the dead shielding skin. That skin helps keep the area clean and your body will fight infection and promote healing more efficiently from behind this skin.

A healthy blister does not smell bad and does not discharge very much – if at all. A bad odour and/or pus are signs of infection and necessitate further attention. Treat by applying a stronger antiseptic solution, and more frequent clean dressing changes.

If your decision is to walk to safety in a survival situation, prepare your feet and boots as well as possible before you depart. Take any available foot care first-aid supplies with you.

Chafes can vary from irritating to debilitating and can ruin your day walk or be a severe setback to your plans on an extended walk.

To reduce the possibility of chafes, wear natural lightweight fabric trousers that are loose fitting in the crutch area. Wear a good belt that supports your trousers and won't allow them to slip down as you walk, or with weight loss. Avoid tight-fitting jeans on long walks and wear underwear made mainly out of cotton.

If a chafe starts, remove your underwear and walk on without them. You can apply a wide Hypafix dressing over a developing chafe – this does alleviate a lot of the painfulness when walking.

Personally, when I am on a long a walk I wear 'fireman's' 50-millimetre-wide trouser braces to prevent crutch chafing and keep the belt pressure off my stomach. It also stops my pants from causing resistance when I need to raise my leg while ascending steep slopes.

 **OWL WISDOM:** **Severe blisters and chafes can slow your walking speed down to 500 metres per hour. This will in turn cause leg muscles to cramp and you will be in deep trouble in the ability-to-move department – this could cause your demise.**

# PART 3
# APPENDICES

# YOUR EMERGENCY CONTACTS LIST

In a life-threatening situation call **000**. That number has a stronger reception signal over our normal mobile phone reception or service range.

Phone a friend. Have a list of your friends or work colleagues who could assist you if it is not a life-threatening situation.

For directory assistance for any phone number dial 1234 and they can either connect you directly or give you the number.

Below are some phone numbers that can assist you in life-threatening or first-aid situations. This is by no means a complete list but may help in the compilation of your own emergency contacts list.

| Life-threatening emergencies only: | | 000 |
|---|---|---|
| Call Connect – National: | | 1234 & 12456 |
| Health direct – 24-hour GP health advice: | | 1800 022 222 |
| Poisons Information Centre – National: | | 13 11 26 |
| Royal Flying Doctors Service WA 24-hour medical and emergency calls. | | 1800 625 800 |
| RFDS Satellite phone calls WA: | | 08 9417 6389 |
| Royal Flying Doctors Service SA & NT 24-hour service. | | 08 8648 9555 |
| Royal Flying Doctors Service QLD 24-hour service. | | |
| Charleville Base | | 07 4654 1443 |
| Mt Isa Base | | 07 4743 2802 |
| Cairns Base | | 07 4040 0500 |
| Royal Flying Doctors Service NSW, VIC, TAS 24 hour service. | | 08 8088 1188 |
| Rescue Coordination Centre (RCC) – Australia 24-hour emergency numbers: | Maritime | 1800 641 792 or +612 6230 6811 |
| | Aviation | 1800 815 257 or +612 6230 6899 |
| Important information on Search and Rescue coordination is available at www.amsa.gov.au/Search_and_Rescue/ Important information on distress beacons is available at http://beacons.amsa.gov.au/ | | |
| Bureau of Meteorology recorded messages for cyclone warnings: | | |
| Tropical Cyclone Warnings (WA): | | 1300 659 210 |
| Tropical Cyclone Warnings (NT): | | 1300 659 211 |
| Tropical Cyclone Warnings (QLD): | | 1300 659 212 |

These lists are correct at the time of writing. Update your personal emergency contact list regularly.

# BUSHFIRE AND FLOOD WARNINGS

ABC radio stations are our emergency broadcasters for natural disaster warnings, with a network of more than 60 stations throughout Australia. ABC Local Radio is uniquely placed to communicate emergency updates to communities affected by natural disasters. Tune in for information, advice and updates and act immediately on the advice provided.

Mobile phones: use your mobile phone device to stay up to date with emergency information and alerts, for example ABC News. Emergency agencies are also developing a range of mobile apps to keep you informed.

# ROAD CONDITIONS

A sudden downpour of rain may cause flash floods that fill up the creek crossings. This happens not only in tropical areas, but also in the normally arid central and southern regions. Before setting off on a journey over unsealed roads, check conditions with local road-report services, as some roads could be closed to all traffic. Local shires have road conditions updated on a daily basis.

# HELPFUL HINTS

To call out of Australia: dial 0011 then the country number followed by the phone number, leaving out the first zero of the area code.

To call into Australia: dial out of your country, then 61, then the phone number, leaving out the first zero from our state or territory code.

To phone a mobile from overseas, dial out of that country, then 61, then the mobile phone number, leaving out the first zero. (In Australia 'cell' phones are commonly referred to as mobile phones or mobiles.)

## Safe travels.

# ACKNOWLEDGEMENTS

This list of acknowledgements does not do justice to the numerous people – from all walks of life, countries and cultures – who have helped me physically, mentally and spiritually over many years to become the person and teacher that I am today. Special people in my life have been my mother Mary Cooper, David Giddens, David Alloway, Blue Morris, Janet Johnson, Bob Hunter, Michael House, Caroline Amos, Carol de Leeuw, Sid de Burgh, David Stiff, Kim Akerman, Oyers Panders, Graham Brammer, Christine Hammond, Greg Winter, Ronnie and Will Atkins, Vanessa Paget, Rich Hungerford, Peter Hickey, Ian and Val Dunnet, Bruce Russell, Rod Chapman, Hugh Brown, and the countless, countless other people of the world who have either supported or guided me through my life. To them all, I say thank you.

Special thanks to Dr Lt Col Graeme Hammond, Senior Medical Officer, Special Operations Command in Australia, for the years of guidance and his support for this book. Also special thanks to Lazar Radanovich for his wonderful illustrations and Sangi for her technical advice.

Bob Cooper

# INDEX